LECRETIA'S CHOICE

In 2015 Matt Vickers supported his wife, Lecretia Seales, in her campaign to gain the right to choose how she died. *Lecretia's Choice* is his first book.

For more information, please visit lecretia.org.

Facebook: facebook.com/lecretiaschoice
Twitter: @lecretiaschoice

Lecretia's choice

A story of love, death and the law

Matt Vickers

TEXT PUBLISHING MELBOURNE AUSTRALIA

textpublishing.com.au

The Text Publishing Company
Swann House
22 William Street
Melbourne Victoria 3000 Australia

First published in 2016 by The Text Publishing Company

Cover photograph by Matt Vickers
Cover design by Text
Page design by Jessica Horrocks

Printed in Australia by Griffin Press, an Accredited ISO AS/NZS 14001:2004 Environmental Management System printer.

National Library of Australia Cataloguing-in-Publication entry
Creator: Vickers, Matt, author.
Title: Lecretia's choice: a story of love, death and the law/by Matt Vickers.
ISBN: 9781925355598 (paperback)
ISBN: 9781925410020 (ebook)
Subjects: Seales, Lecretia. Brain—Tumors—Patients—New Zealand—Biography. Right to die—Moral and ethical aspects. Assisted suicide—Moral and ethical aspects. Euthanasia—Law and legislation—New Zealand.
Dewey Number: 362.196994810092

This book is printed on paper certified against the Forest Stewardship Council® Standards. Griffin Press holds FSC chain-of-custody certification SGS-COC-005088. FSC promotes environmentally responsible, socially beneficial and economically viable management of the world's forests.

In memory of my beloved wife,
Lecretia Anne Seales
1973–2015

With respect and love to the families of Brittany Maynard, Robin Stransham-Ford, Gloria Taylor, Diane Pretty, Marie Fleming, Sue Rodriguez, Chantal Sébire, Ramón Sampedro, Terry Pratchett and the many, many others who overcame their suffering to campaign and fight for modern and compassionate assisted-dying laws on behalf of all of us.

Chapter 1

I WILL ALWAYS remember the sense of surprise and intensity of feeling when I first went out with Lecretia.

I had met her three days earlier. It was a Friday evening. I'd gone to an ex-girlfriend's farewell party at Hummingbird, a bar on Courtenay Place in Wellington. My ex was moving back to Greece to start a job there. It was 7 July 2003 and I rather hoped she might return my Smiths CDs. I took a friend along with me, a guy named Rodney who drew cartoons.

I remember being immediately drawn to a woman sitting at the long table by the window. It was an hour past sunset, and the last light from behind the horizon was sustained by the glow of the streetlights. She was sitting with a group of girlfriends who were in animated conversation. She would interject now and then, but mostly she smiled and laughed. She wore a stylish leather jacket and her hair was tied in two braids. Her smile was generous and she was extraordinarily beautiful.

A waitress passed by me with a plate of thin fries balanced on a tray, clearly bound for these young women. As she passed, I reached out on a whim and took one, without the waitress noticing, and ate it, smiling at the braided woman as I did so.

This got their attention. They called out to me in indignation and I wandered over, apologising. 'I'm sorry, I couldn't resist.' Bolstered by several beers' worth of courage, I sat down and introduced myself. I was still about three chairs away from the braided woman, who was clearly amused by me but didn't say very much. I stole glances at her as I talked to one of her friends. I learned that the women were mostly workmates from a Wellington law firm. They were all drinking champagne.

Now my friend Rodney joined us and we proceeded to banter with the girls. To my annoyance, Rodney sat next to the braided girl and was soon deep in conversation with her. After some time, and feeling envious, I reminded him that we were expected at another bar.

'I kind of had my eye on her,' I said, once we were out on the street.

'All's fair in love and war, mate. She gave me her card.'

'Seriously?'

At the new bar I tried to converse with Rodney's friends, but I couldn't take my mind off the woman at Hummingbird. After a drink or two, I slipped out unnoticed and headed back to Courtenay Place.

The girls were still there and I joined them, offering some excuse for Rodney's absence as I sat down next to the braided girl. We started to talk. She was a lawyer from Tauranga, in the Bay of Plenty, and her name was Lecretia. 'That's a lovely name,' I said. She was tipsy, and so was I. And somehow, over several drinks, we ended up kissing there in the bar, in front of her amused friends and colleagues.

My phone beeped. It was a text from Rodney: 'Where are you?'

'All's fair in love and war,' I texted back.

I was still kissing Lecretia when Rodney arrived back at the bar. At this point Lecretia's friends had decided it was time to move on. We went around the corner to another bar on the pretext of dancing, but all that happened was I ended up kissing Lecretia some more. Finally Lecretia's friends decided it was time to call it a night. They piled into a cab, and Rodney and I hopped into a taxi up to Mount Victoria, in search of another party.

*

I woke the next day with a hangover, and thinking of Lecretia—who was that girl I'd kissed last night? I had enjoyed kissing her so much. I was already smitten.

I didn't know her last name, so I googled her. 'Lecretia, lawyer, wellington.' I found her almost immediately. Lecretia Seales was an associate at Chen Palmer & Partners in Wellington. I looked at her picture. She was as beautiful as I remembered. I needed to see her again. But her contact details weren't on the website.

I called Rodney, remembering he had her card. 'I need Lecretia's contact details.'

'I'm still upset with you.'

'Look, I need to ask this girl out. We kissed. If she says no, you can ask her out.'

'You owe me one,' he said.

Now I had her work number and her email address. On Sunday, after I had recovered from my hangover, I decided to write to her.

hello lecretia ...

we met on friday, at hummingbird ... we were all very badly behaved and i am sure that if there is an afterlife, we will be called to account for it ... after i left you outside hummingbird, i went to a party in mt. victoria somewhere where i tried to convince the revellers that i was an idiot savant ... it didn't really work out ... in the morning (or rather, early afternoon), i awoke with a splitting headache and a great deal of moral guilt ... but that's bohemianism for you ... it's all about the present, and never the consequences ...

speaking of consequences: the consequence of giving me your business card is this missive ... i would like the chance to meet you in a less bacchanalian environment ... i'm not normally so crass and bold ... i am usually a gentle creature of forethought and passion ... well, maybe ...

do you have a cellular phone by which i could reach you? ... i could call you at work, but i would prefer not to ...

in any case, it was a pleasure to meet you ... i hope to hear from you ...

matt

At the time I was halfway through a writing degree, and my supervisor still had some way to go to knock all of the pretentiousness out of me. I thought the use of lower case and ellipses to string fragments of sentences together was very sophisticated—as though I was too nonchalant and freewheeling for the jolt of a full stop. And of course she hadn't given me her business card—she'd given it to Rodney. I hoped she wouldn't remember that detail.

A few hours later I called her work number, too, not expecting her to answer it on a Sunday. But she did answer. Lecretia was in her office, perhaps as penance for her Friday night.

'Hello, is Lecretia there?'

A pause. 'Speaking.'

'Hi, it's Matt. We met on Friday.'

'Yes, I remember.'

'How are you? I had a bit of a hangover yesterday.'

'So did I. I blame you for that.'

'Well, in my defence, you were well on your way before I arrived.'

'Hmph.'

'I sent you an email.'

'Yes, I saw it.'

'I would really like to see you again.'

'Would you?'

'I would. How about tomorrow night? Let's have a quiet drink and see how it goes.'

A pause again. 'I'm not sure that's a good idea.'

'I'm not like this usually, and I'm sure you're not either. Why don't we just see? What have you got to lose?'

One more pause. 'Okay.'

'Great! I'll email you tomorrow with details. Looking forward to it!'

'Bye.'

'Bye!'

I decided to take her to a tapas bar in the centre of Wellington. I couldn't believe she'd agreed. I wore jeans and a new shirt with hand-painted leaves on it. I was more excited than I had been about any date in a long time.

I was the first to arrive. When Lecretia appeared, I was taken aback at how beautiful she was. She had long brown hair, tan skin, beautiful eyes and the sunniest smile you'd ever seen. She was still dressed in her office clothes, and it being winter she was wearing a long coat. Though she was demurely dressed, her allure was hard to conceal. Her complexion suggested an exotic heritage. Was she Italian, or Spanish, or Māori? I was intrigued.

We sat in the back of the bar, and after some awkward chat about Friday night, we began to talk. It turned out Lecretia was older than me. She had just turned thirty, while I was twenty-six.

Lecretia had grown up in Tauranga, the eldest child born to young parents, Larry and Shirley, with two younger siblings, Jeremy and Kat. They weren't wealthy, but they were a loving family, and Lecretia's parents made all the sacrifices they could for their children's education. Her family came from English and German stock, with a dash of Irish, but there was also Fijian blood, and along the line a Cuban sailor of Spanish extraction.

She excelled at school, and came to Victoria University in Wellington to study law, where she also shone. She specialised in public and constitutional law. She told me about her lecturers, the most formidable being Sir Geoffrey Palmer, the former Labour prime minister. Sir Geoffrey had a seating plan for the lecture theatre and knew exactly where everyone was sitting, so that he could question particular students and reprimand them if they hadn't done their reading.

After three years as a young solicitor at Kensington Swan, she left for London in early 2000. She worked there for a couple of years, and travelled widely in Europe. Back in New Zealand she secured a role at Chen Palmer & Partners, a boutique public law firm started by Sir Geoffrey and Mai Chen, also a former law lecturer. Sir Geoffrey saw Lecretia's potential and took her under his wing. She became one of his associates, a role in which she flourished.

I shared her modest beginnings, having grown up in the poorest suburbs of 1970s Gisborne and later on the outskirts of Napier, a few hours' drive south-east of Tauranga. My father was a joiner, making cabinets and furniture. He was a talented woodworker, and built two of his own houses. He later joined the public service as a property valuer. After my mother had me, she stopped working as an office assistant and became a homemaker, raising me and my younger sister, Natalie.

Where Lecretia had pursued the law, I pursued literature. Though she was only three-and-a-half years older than me, she seemed privy to truths I had yet to encounter, and I found her aura of worldly experience captivating.

Like me, Lecretia wasn't the sort of person to go on about whatever popped into her head. She was a quiet and considered conversationalist who enjoyed the thoughtful exchange of opinions and ideas. Her taciturn nature made her all the more alluring; getting to know her was like investigating a mystery I would never quite be able to solve, no matter how many questions I asked.

I took a chance and asked her to dinner that night, expecting this intriguing woman who was clearly out of my league to say no, but she said yes. We wandered down the street to a Mexican restaurant, and ate quesadillas and drank mescal. We went from there to Good Luck, one of my favourite bars at the time. I flirted with her in earnest there, teasing her and letting her tease me.

Afterwards we walked down to the waterfront. It was a crisp, cold, clear winter night and the stars were out and shining. She was smiling, snug in her overcoat, and her bright eyes shone in the darkness. I took a chance and kissed her, and to my delight she responded. Then she pulled away, protesting that she had work tomorrow, but thanking me for the evening. I stood and watched her walk away. I was so incredulous that this exceptional woman had let me kiss her again that I began to wonder what was wrong with her. My lips tingled with the touch of hers and my breath steamed in the cold air.

Chapter 2

WE TOLD THE story of our first meeting often, and not without embarrassment. Lecretia was a very light drinker, so the way she behaved that night in Hummingbird was completely unlike her. Similarly, locking lips with a stranger was also a first for her. I must have been especially charismatic that night.

In fact, Lecretia told me much later that she had woken with a sense of shame and regret at her uncharacteristic behaviour and vowed never to see me again. That would have been the end of it, had it not been for my email, which she read out to her sister, Kat, over the phone, for her opinion. 'You have to go out with him,' Kat told her. 'He sounds just like you!' That wasn't true, but I am forever grateful to Kat for her urging her big sister to give me a chance.

Lecretia told me she enjoyed our first date. She noticed and liked my shirt with the hand-painted leaves, and she got the impression I was a sharp dresser. 'How was I supposed to know it was the only nice shirt you owned?' she said later. She thought I was funny, and cocky, and confident, which was no doubt overcompensation for the nervousness I felt in her company. Lecretia liked to plan things, so the spontaneity of the date was a welcome break from routine. And inexplicably, she didn't have a boyfriend.

I emailed her the next day:

good morning, gorgeous ... i hope you slept well ...

i had a great time last night ... maybe we could get together again soon? ... i'll be in touch later in the week ...

have a fantastic day!

m.

She replied:

I hope the good morning reference is not an indication that you have only just arisen!

Today is a Red Bull day, which means I'm struggling slightly and need assistance with concentration. Again, I blame you.

I shall look forward to hearing from you.

L

The last sentence sent my heart skipping. Yes, it was precisely the phrase a lawyer would use in speaking to a client, or to someone they were suing, but concealed beneath its stiff formality was a softening of her attitude towards me. She would look forward to seeing me. She would like to see me again.

I wanted to see her again at once, but I held back. I was afraid of scaring her away. My experience with relationships had taught me how precarious these first few days are, that the slightest hint of desperation or overeagerness might be fatal. But I was absolutely enthralled.

When you meet someone truly special, you cannot think of anyone or anything else. Your mind is flooded with new possibilities, new wonders. What might it be like to have dinner with this person? What might it be like to kiss her neck and shoulders? To undress her, to make love to her? To wake up in the morning with her? To climb a mountain with her or visit a foreign city? To be married to her? To have children with her?

You're getting ahead of yourself, but you can't help it—
it's as if you've found yourself on the first couple of pages of
an exciting new book. Where does the story go from here?
You don't know whether the story will have a happy ending,
but right now your heart says: read on, read on.

In Wellington, there was an annual film event called
the Incredibly Strange Film Festival, a curated collection
of films that ranged from schlock, to cult, to camp. I
asked Lecretia along to a 1973 film called *Psyched by the
4-D Witch*, which had a generous write-up in the festival
program. I thought it might make me look sophisticated.

As the lights dimmed and the film started, I put my
arms around Lecretia's shoulders. But the film was terrible.
In Dennis Hopper and Peter Fonda's *Easy Rider*, there is
a famously confronting scene where the protagonists trip
out on LSD in a graveyard. *Psyched by the 4-D Witch* was
like an extended parody of this, using only voiceovers and
stock footage. It dragged on forever.

We were both relieved when the film ended. I was
scared to look at Lecretia because I knew she must have
hated it.

'Do you want to get a cocktail?' I asked.

'Sure,' she said.

We found a bar and ordered.

'Sorry about that,' I said.

'It was *horrible*,' agreed Lecretia. 'It might be the worst film I've ever seen.'

'I enjoyed your company, though. I'll have to choose something much better next time.'

'You will.'

That Friday I met Lecretia for a drink and we talked about our week. We drank a few glasses of wine, ate tapas and talked. This turned out to be a much better plan for a date than attempting to impress her with my esoteric taste in films.

A few dates later Lecretia and I sat in her car outside my place. She was dropping me home. It was dark and the street was clear of traffic. The house loomed up beside me. I kissed her and thanked her for the evening. In the dim light her eyes looked all the brighter.

'Do you want to come in?' I asked.

'I'm not sure,' she said.

'We don't have to rush anything.'

'I know that.'

'I really like you. I'm entranced by you.'

'I like you too. I don't like that you're a smoker, though. I don't date smokers.'

It was true—I had foolishly picked up the habit at university and had yet to shake it.

'I'm flattered that you broke your rules for me,' I said.

'I'm surprised I broke my rules for you.'

'Come in and have a cup of tea,' I said.

She paused. 'Do you have green tea?'

I had my doubts.

'I'm sure we do,' I said.

We walked to my gate and up the stairs. Above the streetlights, the moon was waxing towards full in the sky above Mount Victoria. Lecretia stayed the night. In the morning, I left her asleep in bed, dressed as quietly as I could, and walked down the road to buy croissants and bacon and flowers. I stood on the deck of my flat, overlooking the city, and smoked a cigarette. I made croissants with bacon and brought them in to Lecretia, along with the flowers, and sat with her as we ate them.

'Thank you for staying,' I said. 'I ...'

She smiled.

Being with Lecretia felt natural and inevitable, like destiny. I wanted to spend every night of my life with this girl. I was in heaven.

Lecretia flatted on the other side of town, in Glenmore Street, up in the hills behind Victoria University, where I was doing my writing degree. She lived in a flat with three other early-thirties professionals. After that first night together, our dates frequently ended with us staying at her flat or mine, and the two of us walking together to work in the morning.

Lecretia's flat was behind the botanical gardens. I remember walking through those gardens with her, in late winter, the bare branches of the trees gleaming from the rains that swept through every few days. She showed me her favourite spot, which quickly became mine. There was a point where you descended from a hilly, narrow path into the lower part of the garden, and the path would open out into a clearing, where it forked. A single lamppost, ornate and painted black-green, the sort you would see on an affluent boulevard in a European city, marked the fork. In the early morning you could round the corner of the path and come across this lamppost. Its light would still be on, but the effect would be subtle, washed out by the dawn breaking behind it.

It brought to mind *The Lion, the Witch and the Wardrobe*, where Lucy finds a lamppost and meets Mr Tumnus, the umbrella-bearing faun. Every time we passed that lamppost, it felt like Lecretia and I were embarking on our own adventure. On those walks we'd talk about our plans for the day, and the things we would do to further the projects and challenges in front of us. And then we'd descend into the city, where we parted ways until the stars started coming out.

Lecretia invited me over one night for a dinner party to meet her good friend Tim Clarke and his girlfriend, Sam. Tim was a brilliant young lawyer who was a partner at the leading law firm Russell McVeagh. He'd grown up with modest beginnings in Tauranga too. He was an incredibly polite and considerate man and I was enormously impressed by him.

Not long after, I met Lecretia's parents at her flat. Larry and Shirley were younger than I'd expected—far younger than my parents—and I learned that Shirley had been barely sixteen when she fell pregnant with Lecretia, and Larry not much older. Shirley had come from a tough background, and was responsible for her siblings from a very young age. When her mother died, at just forty-three, Shirley and her sister Lorraine went to a foster home, where they were much better cared for. She was living there when she met Larry, who came from a much bigger family of five brothers and sisters.

They hadn't planned on starting their own family at such an early age, and it could have been a disaster, but Shirley had somehow emerged from her difficult childhood with a vast capacity for love. It may have helped that Larry's family was stable and close-knit. Shirley was adopted as something of a sister to Larry's siblings, and the whole family supported them when their first child, Lecretia, was born in 1973.

Shirley had her daughter's good looks, and she and Lecretia interacted more like sisters than a parent and child. Shirley was quiet but intelligent. Although she had been a bright student, she'd been forced out of school after getting pregnant. A few years later she had gone back to study and graduated with an accounting degree. She was now a director of a significant Tauranga accountancy firm.

Larry, on the other hand, I found slightly intimidating. He was bald, with a greying moustache, and had the physique of a man twenty years his junior. He kept fit by running and playing tennis, and would frequently win championships in his age division at regional and national levels. As someone who found sport almost entirely un-interesting, I must have completely confused him. And yet Lecretia had the same attitude to sport as I did, so perhaps he wasn't all that worried.

Kat, Lecretia's sister, was there too. She struck me as a bit of a wild child. She and her boyfriend were flatting in Wellington and threw a lot of parties. She was almost eight years younger than Lecretia, and she loved and looked up to her big sister.

I didn't get to meet Lecretia's younger brother, Jeremy, that night, but he clearly had a lot in common with Larry. Jeremy was a star footballer until a knee injury had forced him to retire. It would be a few more months until I met him.

The six of us—Lecretia and I, Larry and Shirley, and Kat and her boyfriend—walked from Lecretia's house to a local bistro, where we had dinner and got to know each other. It was clear that Lecretia was something of a golden child—the daughter who had pushed herself to achieve and had found her way in the world with her parents' encouragement and support. She had taken on three jobs simultaneously at high school to pay for her education. She had also entered into a dollar-for-dollar saving scheme with her father to pay for her first year of university. Whatever she saved, he would match. The sum she managed to save caused Larry to spit out his coffee in despair when he heard it, and he never made another deal like that with her again. Instead, Lecretia worked all through her university years, washing dishes and waiting on tables, minimising her student loan borrowings.

After dinner we wandered home. Emboldened by the wine we'd shared, I lit a cigarette.

'He smokes!' called out Shirley, in shock.

Not the best way to endear yourself to your girl-friend's parents.

As much as Lecretia didn't like my smoking she didn't demand that I stop. She did have expectations and standards, however. One night a friend invited me out to her flat-warming. Lecretia was working and couldn't go.

'But come over and stay afterwards. I'm looking forward to seeing you,' she told me.

I went to the flat-warming and ended up drinking too much. Feeling I'd hit my limit, I called a taxi and went home to my flat, without contacting Lecretia at all.

The next morning I got a call from her. 'Where were you last night?'

'I'm sorry, babe. I drank too much, so I came home and crashed. I'm so hung-over.'

'Why didn't you call?'

'I didn't want to talk to you in the state I was in.'

'I waited up for you.' She hung up.

She showed up at my house an hour or two later. We sat on the front porch.

'I'm really disappointed. You don't seem to care about me.'

'I do, of course I do. I just drank too much, I came home and crashed. That's it. I was too tired to call.'

'But you knew I was waiting to hear from you.'

It was our first real fight, and I was to blame. At the time I didn't quite see how. I'd spent so many years being accountable only to myself. And fights usually signalled the end of a relationship. Once it got to fighting, I assumed there was nowhere else for things to go.

After several exchanges, with me saying I'd done

nothing wrong, and Lecretia saying that I'd been selfish and inconsiderate, I said, 'So are you saying you want to break up with me?'

She looked shocked. 'No,' she said. 'Why would I want to do that?'

'Well, you're angry that I didn't call you. I can't change that. So do you want to end things?'

'We're having an argument,' she said. 'I'm disappointed in you. I'm telling you why I'm upset. I just want you to listen and understand, and apologise. I don't want to break up with you.'

'I'm sorry,' I said. 'I should have called you. I was rude not to.'

'Matt, you let me down.'

My parents had kept a quiet peace throughout their marriage—until they didn't. Shortly after the fighting started, the marriage ended. Perhaps I thought marriage wasn't possible when there was disagreement. Perhaps total harmony was the thing I was looking for. But Lecretia taught me that fighting can be constructive and healing. I had wronged her, apologised, and she had forgiven me. We had other fights and disagreements, but I never asked her again if she wanted to end our relationship.

In October 2003, Lecretia found a new flat in Mount Victoria, a short walk from my place. We spent most nights at her house or mine, and in the morning would walk together along the waterfront, past Te Papa and the Civic Square, on the way to work. It was a wonderful time. I was coming towards the end of my masters year, and was working on my folio for hand-in, when my Canadian flatmate suggested we have a Thanksgiving party, since Thanksgiving occurs in October for Canadians. I invited Lecretia, and her first question was what she could bring.

I told her not to worry and just to bring herself.

On the night of the party, I got a text from her. 'I'm downstairs, can you come and help me?'

Lecretia was parked two spaces away from our front door. She was standing beside the car. She greeted me with a hug and a kiss.

'Help me with these, please.'

In the back seat were two enormous platters, piled high with lightly toasted baguette slices, topped with roasted red peppers, basil and feta.

I took one platter, she took the other, and we climbed the stairs back to the flat. I remember being so proud of this gorgeous woman. That night someone took a photo of us both—the earliest photo of the two of us together. We are in armchairs, leaning over the armrests towards each other to fit into the photograph. I wish I had more photos of Lecretia.

Chapter 3

WHEN I FINALLY handed in my writing folio for my masters, Lecretia suggested we go away together. We decided to go to Nelson, a thirty-minute flight from Wellington. Nelson, which is on the South Island, is actually further north than Wellington, on the southern tip of the North Island, and enjoys a much better climate. It is well known for its vibrant arts community.

We stayed at a bed and breakfast, and drank a bottle of expensive champagne to celebrate the completion of my degree. We took a jet boat ride out from the harbour around the coastline of Abel Tasman National Park, where pristine beaches give way to thick native ferns and trees. We circled Split Apple Rock, a neatly bisected boulder whose halves rest in the bay as though on a chopping board.

On that trip Lecretia introduced me to her friend and mentor, Sir Geoffrey Palmer, who lived with his wife Margaret in the hills above Nelson. I was very nervous— Geoffrey was a famous politician and a skilled legislative reformer—but I needn't have worried. Geoffrey was a gracious host and a lively conversationalist. He was curious about me, and my intentions towards Lecretia. He clearly cared about her welfare. After dinner, we wandered back into town. It was a still night. I took a photo of Lecretia and Geoffrey near a waterfront monument. It was a lovely evening. We parted ways and Lecretia and I walked back to our bed and breakfast together.

'He's impressive,' I said. 'I liked him.'

'You were cheeky, asking so many questions. But he liked you, I think.'

'How do you know?'

'I can tell.'

The first year we were together, Lecretia invited me home with her to Tauranga to meet her extended family. She loved these get-togethers. She was the person who always knew whose turn it was to host the Christmas function. It was the sort of thing my family had never had. I wasn't a huge fan of Christmas—my parents split a week before Christmas when I was thirteen—but for

Lecretia, it was the best time of year. It was the time that most reflected her world view: when everyone strove to be selfless, considerate to others, kind. In a way, it was the time of year when other people came closest to her in their own motivations and actions.

We drove up to Tauranga together a few days before Christmas Eve and stayed at Lecretia's parents' home. Once we'd brought our bags into the house, Lecretia flew into activity. She began giving orders in the kitchen, instructed me to decorate the tree, and generally assumed control. But this was merely to prepare for taking things to Auckland, where one of Lecretia's aunties was hosting the day.

I got to meet Jeremy, who had come home from Australia, for the first time. He is a physically imposing figure, with the broad chest and thick thighs of an All Black prop, but he is also a gentle soul, so good-humoured and friendly that he is impossible not to like.

We drove to Auckland on Christmas morning, a three-hour journey. Lecretia and I were crammed together in the back seat of Shirley's car. We arrived shortly after noon.

Lecretia's four aunts adored her, and she adored them. To the eldest, Pat, and her husband, Ron, she was like the daughter they never had, unofficial sister to their three sons. To Angela, she was a treasured niece and role model to her daughters Alex and Meredith. To Soraya, she was close enough in age to be like a little sister. And for Debra, she could do no wrong. Lecretia loved them all equally.

As it happened, Christmas that year was to be hosted by Debra. Debra lived on Auckland's North Shore, and we were among the last to arrive, so I was thrown immediately into meeting Lecretia's extended family. I was welcomed, entertained, plied with alcohol, interrogated, and assessed for suitability all at once. I was terrified, but responded as politely as I could.

After Christmas, Lecretia and I drove up to the Coromandel Peninsula to spend New Year's with some friends of hers at a bach near Matapaua Bay. New Zealand summers can be variable but that year the sun shone day in and day out. Lecretia loved summer, and it loved her. Even the harsh New Zealand sunlight wouldn't burn her, choosing to darken her skin instead. I was blissfully besotted with her. We swam in the surf, and embraced and kissed in the water. We slept in the afternoons. I could make her laugh—I loved her laugh. Her friend Sonya, who we were staying with, commented that I must be good for her, as she'd never seen her laugh as much.

On New Year's Eve we were drinking beers at a beach party at a neighbouring bach. At midnight I finished my last cigarette and threw the rest of the packet into a lit brazier. I hadn't planned to give up, but being with Lecretia, meeting her wonderful family, her kind friends, seeing what a great person she was, I wanted to be a better person. My smoking was stupid. So I gave up that night. I have occasionally smoked the odd cigarette since during a night out, but I've never resumed the habit. And Lecretia was delighted with me.

On the way back to Wellington from the Coromandel, we returned to Tauranga for the marriage of one of Lecretia's best friends, Hilary. It was the first wedding we attended together. Lecretia was a bridesmaid, and she wore a beautiful red dress for the occasion.

After dinner Lecretia's friend Angela took me aside. She was another lawyer, short, blond and fiery, who adored Lecretia and was protective of her. Angela had married a blind man, Ben, a very successful public servant in the education sector.

'It's so nice to meet you finally,' said Angela.

'And you,' I said. 'I heard you weren't too keen on me when Lecretia first started seeing me.'

It was true—Lecretia had told me that Angela had advised her to have her fun but not to get too involved with me, as she thought the age gap was too much for us to surmount.

'I've revised my view,' she said. 'I'm happy you're with Lecretia. But you need to treat her well. She likes you a lot. She thinks you're the one.'

'She thinks I'm the one?'

'Yes.'

It was a lot to think about. How do you know when you've found the person you're supposed to spend the rest of your life with? My relationship with Lecretia was by far the longest and the most successful I had ever been in, but I hadn't given much thought to its future. I was still living in the present.

'I'm flattered,' I said. 'Why hasn't she told me that?'

'She doesn't want to scare you. I'm telling you because you need to decide whether you feel the same way. It wouldn't be fair to lead her on. She'll want marriage and kids soon. If you're not up for that, you should give her the space to find someone who is.'

The thought of Lecretia marrying someone else and having their children filled me with dread.

I found Lecretia and whisked her away from the wedding party to the dance floor. I imagined being with this girl forever and growing old with her. I began to warm to the idea that perhaps being with one person wasn't as frightening as it seemed—that love, though a commitment, was paradoxically a liberation. I smelled her hair and kissed her cheek. Lecretia was the woman for me.

A few months after arriving back in Wellington, I was pondering my next move. I had finished my masters, and was back at work, without really being clear where my work was leading me. Lecretia was absorbed by her job at Chen Palmer & Partners—we would frequently meet at 7.30 pm or 8 pm after she had finished for the day to have a drink or a meal.

Later, when I was back at her house, I would look at the photographs on her walls and in frames on her dresser while she got ready for bed. They were scenes from her life in London, or having fun with friends in Egypt or Naples or Cappadocia. I admired her photographs. She had taken many when she was overseas and had compiled two carefully curated albums of her travels. These were shot on film, developed and neatly adhered to cardboard pages and covered with thin, clear plastic. She treasured these albums and delighted in showing me photos of all the countries she'd visited.

Possibly she had cause to regret her enthusiasm. Unlike so many of my friends, I had not lived or travelled much overseas at all.

I began to talk to Lecretia about my growing urge to

travel. Did she want to come with me? I couldn't bear the idea of breaking up with her, of her finding someone else and starting a life with them.

She said that, although she would miss me, she would understand if I had to go, but she couldn't come with me. She was committed to her job at Chen Palmer & Partners, which was taking off, and being a bit older than me she felt that it was time to be focusing on her career. Later I would find out that she really didn't want me to go—but she didn't want to hold me back either. She didn't want to be the sort of person to hold someone back from their ambitions.

I suppose in a way I was also testing my feelings. Part of me distrusted myself and the future that was becoming clearer and clearer: the life-on-rails that began with birth and inexorably led to marriage, children and death. My thinking was likely influenced by the premillennial angst that spilled over into the early 2000s, the angst that found its origins in Nirvana's *Nevermind* and gave rise to *Fight Club* and *The Beach* and *No Logo* and Radiohead's *OK Computer* and was captured archly in the title of the Strokes' debut album, *Is This It*.

I booked a flight for a three-month round trip to the United Kingdom via Thailand, with the idea I would spend a month backpacking around Thailand, and then get to the UK and decide what to do. Maybe I would stay, get a visa, get a job. I didn't know. I was twenty-seven. I wanted to feel free: to feel like I was making a choice about my future.

Despite not wanting me to go, Lecretia supported me. She helped me pick out a backpack, and she bought a small New Zealand flag patch and sewed it on for me. She bought me a Lonely Planet guide, and offered to look after my belongings. She kissed me goodbye at the airport, and embraced me, making me promise to write to her and call her.

I arrived in Bangkok and made my way to Khao San Road, 'the centre of the backpacking universe', and began to fall into a rhythm of bus trips and beaches and beer and books and conversations with strangers. I travelled to Ko Tao in the Gulf of Thailand and north to Chiang Mai and Pai near the Myanmar border. I learned to dive. I learned to massage. I had *Lost in Translation*-style evenings where I careened headlong through the city, drunk in a taxi with drunk locals I'd met at a noodle house, going from one bar to another, while the lights of the city reflected off every shining surface, before the thud of nightclub music gave way to the thud of a midday headache.

I got to the UK and, after a few days, went to Ireland. I explored Dublin and joined the centennial Bloomsday celebrations. I travelled to the south of France to stay with an ex-flatmate and her family. I ate in spectacular restaurants and explored castles and caves, and kayaked down the Dordogne.

All this time I corresponded with Lecretia, and recounted my adventures to her. She patiently read my emails and responded with concern, and excitement, and wonder. We talked about how much we missed each other.

When I got to France, she emailed me to say that she'd bought a house. She was very excited. She asked me to move in with her when I came home.

> I really love it, Matt. It's not big, and it's not flash, and it is in the suburbs, but it is cute and there is very little that needs doing to it. The grounds are really tidy and it already has a garage. It would be even better with French doors and a deck off the lounge. It would not be too expensive to get a builder to do that sometime. Other than that, we really just need to change the curtains.

I was growing more and more certain that I would return home to her, and that I would choose her as she'd chosen me. But I resisted saying when. I called her from France, excited about the new house, but not promising to be home at the end of July. There were places I still wanted to see.

She wrote me an email the next day, expressing frustration.

> I'm sorry if you thought that I gave you a hard time on the phone. I don't think you understand quite how much the indeterminacy of your trip goes against my grain. I know exactly what I have on every day for the next month. I love that. I love looking at my diary every day and planning my week. I am really struggling with the whole uncertainty of when/if you are coming home. I will deal with it, though. I'm not going to try and factor you into my moving equation now. I'm moving on 24 July. Mum and Dad have kindly said that they will come down and help me.

I replied:

> I know it's hard for you to deal with me being away for an indeterminate amount of time. I could give you answers but you don't seem to like it when I change my mind a week later, which does happen. I am vacillatory by nature, but you must know this already. Nevertheless, there are some facts which I am now unwavering on. These are:
>
> - I love you.
> - I am coming home.
> - I am moving in with you.

The more I travel, the more I want to come home. You worry that I'll find a place that I want to live more than home. That's silly, because all the places that I travel won't have you in them, and to me you're the greatest wonder of the world. I love you, Lecretia. I've never loved anyone as much as I love you.

After Europe, I returned to Asia, for the last leg of my trip. I travelled to Siem Reap in Cambodia and watched the sun set on Angkor Wat from Phnom Bakheng. I took a riverboat through floodplains to Battambang and a motorbike to Pailin on the Thai border where the last vestiges of the Khmer Rouge persisted. I ate croissants and drank beer with prostitutes in Phnom Penh before crossing the border to Vietnam.

In Ho Chi Minh City I played pool against locals in bars while the sound system blared Hendrix and 'Paint It Black'. I bussed north through Nha Trang and Hoi An and Hue, exploring temples and tailors and little restaurants with the freshest spring rolls I'd ever tasted, and I rode taxis in Hanoi watching families piled high on their scooters—five to a seat, plus a couple of chickens. I kayaked through the limestone islands of Ha Long Bay, through caves and floating villages and beneath limestone cliffs where monkeys screeched from the clifftops.

But now I wanted to get home. I had made my choice. I had a photo of Lecretia on my digital camera that I kept looking at. I emailed her.

> I'm starting to miss you like crazy. I think of you all the time: dressed in your beautiful clothes, with your gorgeous smile, or naked in candlelight, or in the morning. How it feels to kiss you. That photo I have I keep returning to, and I want to crawl beneath the little screen and be there with you. I imagine what it will be like when I arrive home, and I wonder whether you will be at the airport waiting for me, and what you will be wearing, and whether I'll cry, or you'll cry. Will I rest my hand on your thigh as you're driving? Will you make me drive instead? Will we go home at once? Will we make love immediately, or will I massage you first? Will I undress you slowly, or hurriedly? If I undress you too fast, will you flash with anger and declare in your Lecretia's-angry voice for me to 'Slow down!'? Will you kiss me at two in the morning, unable to sleep? Will your eyes spring open at 5 am, like they often do, and will you lie awake and listen to me breathing until I finally wake up at 9 am? Will we stay in bed until noon, talking and holding each other and eating chocolates and breakfast and making love?

I miss you so much. I can't wait to see you when I get off that plane.

I will be home soon. I love you, you adorable, exceptional, unique and spectacular woman.

The day finally came when I took my flight from Hanoi back to Wellington via Bangkok. I'd worn the same clothes for three days straight, so I smelled terrible and was unshaven. I pitied those people who had to sit next to me on the plane.

After sixteen hours of travel I disembarked and walked into the arrivals hall.

Lecretia was there waiting for me, her beautiful smile, tears in her eyes, her chestnut-brown hair loose against her shoulders and back. I broke into a trot and closed the distance between us, and took her into my arms, feeling the warmth and give of her body, burying my face in her hair, and then kissing her on her sweet, familiar lips. Seeing her after three months sent a bolt of happiness through me.

She pulled her head away from me, while holding my embrace.

'Pooh! You smell terrible!'

The home Lecretia had chosen was just as she'd described. It was small and elegant. It was perfect. With a mix of nervousness and pride she showed me around: the kitchen, the lounge, the bathroom, the bedroom.

I peeled off my clothes and climbed in the shower, and then Lecretia and I made love for the first time in our new abode. I was so happy, and so was she.

Before my trip around Asia, there was an unanswered question: would this be permanent? Now all the doubt was gone. It would.

Chapter 4

WE BECAME DE FACTO partners, living together, going to work together, spending weekends together. We'd go to garden stores on the weekend and pick out plants and take them home and do our best to keep them alive despite our poor gardening skills. We'd have dinner parties. We'd dress together, have nights out, sleep in together.

It wasn't all rosy. Lecretia confided in friends that living with me was hard—she felt I wasn't pulling my weight. I tried to keep on top of the dishes, the lawns, the rubbish, the domestic routines that come with home ownership. We tussled over who should do what, and when, and what expectations we had of one another.

I took a couple of months to find work, not sure what I wanted to do next. I eventually took a job at a PR company, for no other reason than that it sounded interesting, and started there as an account manager.

Lecretia cooked a lot, even when I wasn't working. She was a talented chef. I had never met someone with so many cookbooks. She had *Culinaria Italy* and *Larousse Gastronomique* and a pasta-maker and a lemon zester and one of those blending wand things. Our cupboards quickly became stocked with spices and preserves and sauces and chocolate and blanched almonds and dried fruits and three different kinds of olive oil, and our fridge with chutneys and capers and cornichons and four different kinds of cheese. How Lecretia found time to do her job and still come home and cook for us always amazed me.

I cooked too, but I stuck to tried and tested dishes. Lecretia patiently (and sometimes less patiently) helped me improve my technique in the kitchen. She showed me the best way to chop tomatoes and onions, impressed upon me the importance of rinsing rice before boiling it in water and letting it simmer on a low heat. My cooking slowly improved.

We made adjustments to the house, adding the deck that Lecretia had envisaged along with French doors. When the sun was out in Wellington, which wasn't as often as we would have liked, Lecretia would spend her afternoons lying out on the deck in a bikini with a book in hand, a bowl of cherries in easy reach. On a still evening we'd sit out in the dusk together and share a glass of wine. We took a holiday in Laos and figured out that we could happily travel together. We began making inquiries about a kitten from breeders of Abyssinian cats. We worked late and came home and laughed together. Making Lecretia laugh was as intoxicating to me as any drug. It was strangely validating: this beautiful woman found me amusing and enjoyed my company. I still couldn't quite believe it.

My decision to propose in July 2005 was an impulsive one. I noticed that the second anniversary of our first date was coming up, and in the absence of any other extraordinary ideas, I thought that popping the question was the best way to make her night memorable. It was an obvious next step, really. Lecretia and I had now been living together for twelve months, and we were in bliss.

The day before our anniversary, Lecretia was working late at Chen Palmer & Partners, preparing for a trip to Auckland the next day. I called her at work after midnight and told her to come home. She told me she just needed another hour. She got home at 3 am, had a couple of hours' sleep, and got up at 5 am to get her taxi to the airport.

I'd booked dinner for us that evening at the White House, a swanky restaurant in Oriental Bay on the eastern edge of the CBD. We'd agreed that Lecretia would come straight from the airport after Auckland and we'd go to dinner to celebrate our anniversary.

I didn't buy a ring—I knew Lecretia would want to choose her own—so there wasn't a hot circle of metal burning in my pocket, just a single question burning in my heart.

I arrived at the White House and was shown to our table. It was covered in a beautiful white cloth, and a single rose rested in a vase in the centre. From my seat, I looked out on a view of the harbour as the sun reddened low in the sky.

'My girlfriend's on her way—she's coming from the airport.'

Almost immediately I received a text message. 'Flight delayed—will be there as soon as I can.'

It's a one-hour flight from Auckland and a ten-minute cab ride from the airport, so things weren't looking good. I ordered a beer and looked out at the slate-blue harbour. The tables around me were full, and I could feel the eyes of the other diners on me and their quiet sympathy. Perhaps I should have got up and gone for a walk. Instead, I sat there and thought about Lecretia.

Somehow I'd found myself with someone who loved me, who was willing to make sacrifices to be with me and who I adored utterly. I felt gloriously out of my depth. I had spent a lot of my youth seeking validation—that I was smart, that I was sexy, that I was loved—and here was a girl who could give me all of that with one glance. I was so happy.

And she was so late. It was 9.30 pm. People were finishing their meals and leaving the restaurant. I must have looked ridiculous at that table, with my beer and my rose and my stupid smile.

'Sir, I'm afraid the kitchen is closing,' the waitress said.

'Right.'

'Is she far away?'

'I think she's still on her flight.'

'I'm afraid we won't be able to serve you tonight.'

'I understand. Can I take this?' I asked, pointing at the rose.

'Sure,' she smiled.

I descended the stairs and began walking into town. My phone rang.

'Hey, Lecretia.'

'I've just landed. I'm so sorry. Are you still at the White House?'

'They're closing. I'm heading into town.'

'Do you still want to go out?'

'Of course. Let's meet at Chow,' I said, choosing an up-market Asian restaurant with one of the town's more exclusive bars attached.

'Okay—I'm getting in a cab. Can't wait to see you!'

Clutching the rose, and spurred on by the cold winter air, I started running. I ran along the footpath that traced around the outline of the harbour, past the million-dollar houses that terraced their way back up the hill, and into the amber haze of the streetlights of Courtenay Place, where we had first met. I ran around the corner into Tory Street, and was outside Chow when Lecretia pulled up two minutes later in her cab. She stepped out, looking tired but beautiful. She was crying.

I hugged her and held her.

'I'm sorry,' she said. 'There was fog that delayed the plane for two hours.'

'It's okay. Let's go upstairs.'

We approached the maître d' and asked for a table. He took us to the back of the restaurant, a small two-seater table, and we looked at our menus.

'How are you feeling?' I asked. 'You must be exhausted. Did the meeting go well?'

'I think so.'

My heart was beating fast. I was determined to ask.

I held on for the right moment. The waiter took our orders and shortly the food arrived: dumplings and satay and salad and fish cakes to share.

I picked up a peanut and blue cheese wonton in my chopsticks and bit into it. I swallowed.

'Lecretia, I want to say something.'

She looked at me, a little apprehensively. She held my gaze. She looked beautiful.

'It's our anniversary tonight. It's been two years. We've moved in with each other, and I'm really happy. I love living with you and sharing a bed with you and making love to you. I love it that sometimes you tell me off and that even when I'm an idiot you forgive me and love me anyway. I love how you laugh at my jokes. I love your spectacular boobs. I love your eyes and your smile and the way you make me want to be a better person.'

She continued to look at me, more intently now. She was holding her breath.

'I've given it a lot of thought and I want to ask you something.' I paused. 'Will you marry me?'

I will never forget the smile that broke out, and the utter happiness in her eyes. As for me, I felt dizzy. I felt the entire course of my life shifting. I was excited. I was scared. But I was happy too.

'Yes,' she replied. 'Yes, yes, yes!'

And with that our lives became entwined forever. She leaned across the table and kissed me. The blue cheese wonton dropped from my chopsticks. I returned her kiss, a lover's kiss, oblivious to everyone else in the restaurant.

We laughed and joked over the rest of dinner. I told her about how I'd been sitting at the White House, thinking of her, and how I'd run to Chow. We talked about shopping for a ring. She told me about her day in Auckland. We discussed the pending arrival of our Abyssinian kitten—not quite a baby, but a commitment nonetheless. We paid, and caught a cab home. I took my fiancée's hand and led her to our bedroom. We undressed and kissed and made love and fell asleep in each other's arms. We were in love, and now we were going to be together for eternity.

Chapter 5

IN A NAIVE way, I hadn't anticipated how quickly things would develop after I popped the question.

Lecretia announced her engagement to her colleagues the next Monday and insisted I tell my workmates too. Congratulations started rolling in and so did the questions—when would we be married? Where? Big or small wedding? In New Zealand or overseas? What did the ring look like?

And Lecretia had her own questions too.

'When would you like to get married?'

'I don't see a rush—we just got engaged. Why don't we enjoy that for a while?'

'Oh no,' she said. 'The whole point of getting engaged is to get married. I'm not waiting.'

'So when were you thinking?'

'Early next year.'

'That's only a few months away! I'm still getting used to the idea of being engaged!'

'Well, get used to the idea you're getting married!'

I had unleashed a hurricane of activity. Within two weeks of my proposal my inbox was filled with quotes and estimates from venues and caterers and wedding photographers and florists and cake decorators and more.

I was being asked for my opinion on everything. I had to choose between two shades of green for the invitations. I had to come up with my guest list. I had to choose what flowers I liked. What kind of cake did I want? Which photography package?

I tried to delegate all decisions to Lecretia, but it didn't work. I made the fatal mistake of disagreeing with one of her choices.

'You say you don't want to be bothered with the decision-making,' she declared, 'but then when I choose something you do have an opinion. I need you to participate! This is *our* day!'

We flew up to Tauranga and spent a weekend inspecting churches and venues. We looked at a garden at an architect's house. Two country estates. Two chapels. A winery. Lecretia's dad suggested the Tauranga football club. Lecretia took one look at the place and walked out again.

We finally decided we would be married at St Joseph's Church in Te Puna, a small chapel outside Tauranga. It was a modest wooden church that barely seated 120 people. Behind the altar the words of Christ and God swirled in English and Māori. The church was on a hill a short drive from the coast, and on a sunny day it stood stark against the sky as an unambiguous block of colour, with the clear and confident lines of a Rita Angus painting.

Securing the church was my responsibility. It was a Catholic church, and I was the closest thing to a Catholic out of the two of us. I had the guilt and I had the sin, but I had neither the faith nor the appetite to acquire it. But at least my grandmother, a committed and humble Catholic, would be happy.

For the reception we chose Mills Reef Winery, one of Tauranga's few wineries and likely the best. We set a date of 8 April 2006.

Now everything began to fall into place: the chef, the photographer, the florist, the band. There was no going back.

While we were preparing for the wedding, and after two months of kitten photos, our Abyssinian arrived from the breeder in Christchurch. We decided to call him Ferdinand. He was a tiny bundle of flecked ginger and chocolate fur and he had big green eyes. His tail stood up erect, but the last inch or so was kinked forward at a right angle. After settling in to our home he took to chasing balled-up and discarded drafts of wedding invitations around the room.

Getting married in a Catholic church isn't something you can just do, it turned out. There are rules. Our first appointment was with a priest in Wellington. For our application to be married at the church to be approved, he said, we had to make a promise to do three things.

'What are they?' I asked.

'You need to do a counselling session with a married couple in the community to look at your compatibility.'

'Sure,' I said.

'You need to do a group counselling session with other couples, to learn some tools to be effective in your relationship.'

'Sure,' I said.

'And finally, you need to promise to do your best to bring your children up to know the Catholic faith.'

I was uncomfortable with that promise then, and I am

still uncomfortable with it now. My intent was to raise children who could make their own minds up about the world. But I thought about the wording. I would tell our children what Catholics believe. I would take them to the church to show them. I would even have them baptised as I had been baptised. But I would let them make up their own minds.

'I promise that any children I have with Lecretia will know the Catholic faith.'

And, with that, we had a wedding venue.

Before our first counselling session we were given a questionnaire to answer about our attitudes on everything including domestic duties, sex, children, religion, finances, priorities and work. Our answers were reviewed by a couple who lived close to us, in a beautiful house that oozed tasteful wealth and privilege. The evening we were to see them, we knocked on the door and were invited in to sit down in their living room.

Our counsellors were in their forties. He was a successful senior manager, the sort of clean-living, sober and serious person who rises to become a top public servant or banker. She was a homemaker. And together I supposed they represented the sort of archetypal couple the Catholic Church would hold up as exemplary.

Is this what we were expected to be like? I was terrified.

'We've compared your questionnaires, and tonight we'll go through the results and point out where there are clear differences in your expectations—the purpose being for you to look at those differences and discuss, acknowledge and if possible resolve them.'

And we sat, one couple facing another couple, as they unpicked our relationship and explained how different we were.

Lecretia wanted four kids. I wanted two. She valued having children more than anything else. I valued travel and fun. She felt I didn't do enough around the house. I felt like we were about equal. She saw sex as extremely important; I saw it as moderately important. (That was a surprise.) She equated family with freedom. I equated money with freedom. And on it went.

It was a really useful exercise. There were things that we had never discussed: how we'd share our finances, how we'd school our kids and so on.

The couple showed us to the door and we shook their hands. Walking home, we discussed our evening and the bigger issues. We had a new understanding of each other.

Our next session was a group session over a weekend. We heard from couples who'd been married for decades about the challenges they'd experienced. We learned about the difference between sex and love and the purpose of each. We were given handouts and diagrams. At one point we were asked to hold hands, and to recite the Blessing of the Hands, a meditation about how we would support each other. We both burst into tears.

As we moved steadily towards our wedding, our working lives seemed to take on more urgency. My job at the public relations agency was becoming more demanding. I worked on books and speeches and articles. But I was becoming uncomfortable with the demands of the job. PR is about spin and rhetoric, and convincing people to believe things are important when they aren't, or that they aren't important when they are. It wasn't for me. I lasted less than ten months, and I resigned a few weeks before the wedding.

When I met Lecretia, Chen Palmer & Partners was at the height of its powers. Mai and Geoffrey had turned their firm into a public law machine. All of this meant exciting work, and Lecretia loved it. She often accompanied Geoffrey on visits to parliament or to clients, and he regarded her as an extraordinarily dependable and diligent associate. Lecretia was the soul of discretion, and kept most of the details of her work completely confidential, even from me.

I didn't often see Lecretia on a Wednesday night, as she would regularly accompany Geoffrey to his public law lectures for third year students at Victoria University. Many younger lawyers Lecretia encountered later in her career would remember her quiet presence there as Sir Geoffrey sallied forth from the lectern.

Lecretia had always enjoyed working for Geoffrey. She found him demanding but fair, and able to communicate clearly what he expected from her. But eventually Geoffrey had decided to move on from the firm and pursue other opportunities. As he prepared to go, more of the rain-making fell on the shoulders of Mai, and she began taking on more and more of his team to backfill the work.

After Geoffrey left, so did the rest of the partners, leaving Mai as the sole partner in charge of the firm. The firm's name was shortened from Chen Palmer & Partners to just Chen Palmer. Mai quickly came to rely on Lecretia just as Geoffrey had. Mai could be extraordinarily kind and very generous, but like a lot of brilliant business-people, she worked hard and expected her employees to work just as hard.

Lecretia had always been a hard worker. She worked like she had a personal stake in the company. If she was behind, she would work all hours to catch up, and if she let her employer down she took it as a personal failure.

Knowing Mai needed her, she started working harder than she ever had before.

Lecretia worked right up until a day before the wedding.

On the day of the wedding, my three groomsmen and I got up early and met the photographer, who accompanied us into town for breakfast. I had spent the night in a motel, while Lecretia slept at her parents' home. It was a beautiful Tauranga day and we enjoyed French toast with bacon and champagne by the waterfront. I took the chance to practise my wedding speech.

We were the first to climb the steps to the church. The sun was bright in the sky and the church was resplendent. We stopped to put in our lapel pins.

'Are you nervous?' asked Damian, my best man.

'No,' I said. 'Excited, actually. You've got the ring, right?'

He tapped his pocket. 'Of course. Let's just hope she turns up.'

As guests started arriving I stood at the door of the church welcoming them in. I'd chosen Sigur Rós as the accompaniment to people being seated.

After everyone had taken their seats I resumed my position in front of the chancel. There was still no sign of Lecretia. We stood waiting while Sigur Rós crooned away in inscrutable Icelandic. The attendees were smiling at me and glancing at the door. I saw Lecretia's family and mine, old school friends, work colleagues and others. The church had stained-glass windows which cast rainbow hues over everyone's faces.

At last, one of Lecretia's bridesmaids appeared in the doorway, and began walking down the aisle to a bridal march. Others followed behind her in their maroon dresses, paused, and stepped ceremoniously towards the front, beaming.

And then Lecretia appeared with her father. She was wearing a simple, elegant white dress, no train, her head covered by a veil. My heart leapt when I saw her familiar figure. Her eyes were on me as she walked through the church. When she was almost at the front, I shook Larry's hand and then took Lecretia's, guiding her to stand across from me. I pushed back her veil and she was revealed, her glorious eyes and sweet smile and tender gaze.

Any last lingering doubts or fears melted away in that moment. She looked at me with such trust and acceptance, such love, that I knew I had found someone with whom I could share my life.

We exchanged vows and rings. The priest declared us man and wife. And in that instant, I sensed an infinite number of possibilities winking out of existence, leaving only this woman to whom I had said yes. Lecretia never shone more brightly than that day. I had never been more certain of anything or anyone in my life. We were made for each other. When I kissed her in front of everyone I couldn't have been prouder. She held me tightly and kissed me back.

We walked out of the church into the sunshine. We descended the steps and turned to look up at the narrow doorway of the church as our guests emerged to greet us. In twos and threes they came and shook our hands and kissed our cheeks.

We stood by a green hedgerow while guests were configured and arranged to be photographed with us. Lecretia's family, my family, siblings, cousins—they all had their turn. There was one final shot of us from the doorway of the church, with all our wedding guests behind us, all supporting our union.

Lecretia never sought the spotlight, never wanted to be the centre of attention. But on this day, she embraced it. There was no modesty, no bashfulness. She sparkled like a diamond and smiled and laughed and it was glorious.

Later, after the speeches and the dancing, we were driven into town to the hotel where we would spend the night. We checked in and went to our room. We undressed and made love and lay tangled in each other's arms.

'I know it was our wedding,' said Lecretia, resting her head on my chest. 'But objectively speaking, I think that was the best wedding I've ever been to.'

'I agree,' I said.

I tilted Lecretia's head up and kissed her. And then, in every sense, we were husband and wife.

Chapter 6

OUR MARRIAGE BEGAN with a trip to Cuba. I was curious about the place—the beautiful old American cars, Havana, Hemingway, cigars, mojitos and the mob. Lecretia's reasons for visiting were more personal. Somewhere in her Fijian grandfather's ancestry was a Spanish sailor who came to Fiji via Cuba. She wasn't planning to look up relatives, but she wanted a sense of where she came from.

We flew to Havana via Santiago, and stayed in the city a few days before taking a private tour around the island. Cubans were a fun and friendly people but any appearance of wealth or prosperity was a facade. Behind the gorgeous Spanish edifices in Havana were unfurnished rooms and slums. Under the bonnets of classic cars were Russian parts, the American engines having long since expired. Even the money was an illusion: we used convertible pesos which could only be spent in certain stores, while the Cubans had their own peso.

In the first restaurant we visited, the waiter handed us a menu. We studied it. Five minutes later, he returned.

'I'm sorry, but we're not able to serve anything on the menu today. We have grilled pork, grilled chicken, or grilled fish, with a salad.'

Lecretia and I looked at each other.

'Grilled pork,' I said.

'Grilled fish.'

In a few minutes the waiter returned with two plates, one bearing a single piece of seared fish, with no seasoning. The pork was served the same way. And the salad was slices of raw carrot and slivers of beans.

The meal cost us US$50.

The food didn't improve for the entire trip, but once we understood why—the loss of ties to the Soviet Union, the trade embargoes, the government rationing of food and the high cost of some of the things we took for granted, particularly spices—it made sense. But mojitos—rum, sugar, mint and lime, all of which are plentiful in Cuba—were cheap and delicious.

We headed west to Parque Nacional Viñales, speeding

down motorways past hitchhikers and tobacco plantations. We travelled back east to Trinidad, a town in the centre of the island, where the streets were lined with brightly painted doors. We headed to the resorts of Varadero, stopping for ice cream and passing oil pumps at work on their pivots in brown fields. We spent three days lazing on loungers and drinking cocktails and swimming in the pale blue sea.

It wasn't an easy trip, but it brought Lecretia and me closer together as we relied on each other's limited Spanish. When we returned to Havana, we sat on the Malecón, the esplanade along the coast where desperate Cubans launch their dangerous rafts in search of Florida, and we watched convertible Cadillacs pass by with white-dressed brides sitting up on the trunk with their legs in the back seat.

When we got home it was approaching winter. It was difficult to reacclimatise to the chilly Wellington weather after the tropical temperatures of the Caribbean. And after three weeks in Cuba, where there was no outdoor advertising, the sight of a billboard was jarring. Ferdinand was glad we were back, but he sulked for a while before he forgave us.

We began our lives as a married couple, and it was bliss. We'd ironed out most of the kinks in our domestic arrangements. We went to parties and shows and held dinner parties. I dreamt for her that she would have everything she wanted, and she dreamt the same for me. I have seen marriages where one partner's desires subsume the other's—the more compromising partner gets bound up in the identity of the more dominant partner and loses something of themselves. That didn't happen with us. On the contrary, I think we made each other stronger.

This was reflected in our working lives. I became more ambitious. I was married to someone I respected and admired and I wanted to deserve her love. Lecretia was a high achiever and I felt like I was just starting out. At work, I shifted gears and moved from coding software into business analysis. It taught me to develop new skills: working with clients, solving problems, making presentations and winning new business.

Meanwhile, Lecretia was under extraordinary pressure. She was now effectively the second most senior lawyer in the business. While Mai held the firm together, Lecretia played a key role in advising and supporting her and her staff. Eventually Mai introduced several more senior hires into the team, including a woman named Catherine Marks with whom Lecretia formed a firm friendship. Catherine was a brilliant lawyer, and she and Lecretia worked well together.

I asked Lecretia sometimes whether she believed she should be made partner. She certainly deserved it—she was a first-rate lawyer, liked and respected by her clients, and she worked very hard—but despite her ambition I sensed she was conflicted about it, perhaps because we had recently begun thinking about children. Lecretia wanted children more than anything else, and she was worried that the demands of being a partner might interfere with being a good mother, or being a mother at all.

I've always been good with kids. Play comes naturally to me—I can switch on my imagination and communicate with children at their level. They like me for it. Lecretia wasn't as easy-going around them as I was—she wasn't much for play—but her love, and care, and adoration shone out of her. She loved holding babies, she loved how they smelled and how they would nestle into her for warmth and comfort. I could see that she would be the same sort of mother as her own mother: someone who would show her love through sacrifice, putting her child ahead of herself in all things.

We began trying to conceive naturally. Lecretia was thirty-four and I was thirty-one, so we figured that a few months of trying should be fun and get us results. But within a short period of time the lack of success became stressful. I cut back on alcohol and took care of my diet, and Lecretia plied me with a variety of pharmacological and herbal supplements to supercharge my potency—despite my tests all indicating I had no fertility issues. She too took a cocktail of supplements to boost her own fertility. But the new routines became a burden.

A cycle would begin, and we would try to stay healthy as Lecretia tracked something called the luteinising hormone, waiting for a surge in numbers that appeared a few days before ovulation and marked the optimum time to conceive. As much as I enjoyed making love to my wife, the introduction of a schedule into our sex life felt antithetical to passion. Nevertheless, we'd persist and there would be an anxious two-week wait to see whether we had been successful, during which Lecretia would carefully monitor her diet. She would test herself for pregnancy. Sometimes a promising faint blue line would appear.

The arrival of her period was always heartbreaking for her. Every month she dared to hope, and every month she was let down.

In early 2007, after almost a year with no success, we approached a medical practice that assisted couples in achieving healthy pregnancies. Lecretia and I were tested. The news was bad. She had endometriosis. Her fallopian tubes, instead of being smooth and clear, were striated and distorted. Lecretia described subsequent events in a diary she started after entering treatment.

16 March 2007

Nine days since I was told I have endometriosis and need laparoscopic surgery. I am devastated. I was completely unprepared for this and am surprised by how upset it has made me. It is getting easier to deal with but I am finding it very hard. I told Mai earlier in the week. She was very good about it. She advised me to treat it like a client problem and told me to open a file called BAB100/01! Tonight my new grad (who has two children at twenty-five) asked me if I had children, and then if I wanted them. It really upset me. We had drinks at Mai's and there were children everywhere. I feel very much an outsider at these things.

The purpose of the surgery was to remove as much of the endometriosis as possible, to give her eggs a better chance of reaching the womb. But Lecretia wasn't convinced that the endometriosis was the sole cause of her problems. She started looking at other things in her life that might be contributing to her infertility, and an obvious candidate was work. Lecretia was barely sleeping—she would be home late at night and awake again and in at the office before I'd opened my eyes. She was under a lot of stress, and she'd had a few disagreements with Mai, too.

27 May 2007

The operation went well according to the surgeon, although he said the endometriosis was substantial. The operation was scheduled for the worst possible time with work, which made it more stressful. We didn't try last month, as it was only a week or so after my operation. Matt has been very good about everything. I am lucky to have such a loving and supportive husband. I've had a couple of hideously stressful weeks at work. I don't think I've been this stressed for a long time. I'm feeling much more positive, though. Before I was thinking that we would never have a baby, but now I'm thinking that we will get there. I think it is important for me to get more relaxation time. I wanted a promotion at work, but now I think I have come to the realisation that it is not more important than having a family. Work is causing me a huge amount of stress at the moment, and Matt is bearing the brunt of it, which is unfair. I'm going to try and be much more zen this week. We're going to try again this month naturally and then next month start intra-uterine insemination. It sounds unpleasant, and it is bloody expensive, but we cannot get state-funded IVF until we have done three IUIs. Stupid. Matt's sperm is fine, though, so that's something. It's just me who's defective. I'm anxious that time is slipping away.

I think my disagreement with Mai last week is helping me to realise I need to put other things ahead of my job. It's hard, though. A friend said things would happen when I really wanted them to. Well, I really do.

1 June 2007
I dreamt last night that I had a baby boy. I delivered it myself in bed, but then I didn't know what to do with it. Maybe I think I won't know what to do with one.

17 June 2007
A colleague is pregnant after two months of trying. I'm pleased for her, of course, but it is like a dagger when I have just got my period. Picked up the IUI drugs today. Didn't realise they are injections. Lucky I don't have a needle phobia.

Under New Zealand law, before in-vitro fertilisation or IVF is publicly funded, you must first attempt something called intra-uterine insemination or IUI. In IUI, they take a semen sample, wash the sperm so that only healthy, active sperm remain, then inject the sperm into the uterus. It's the same thing they do with livestock, and it feels that way too.

Even when you're the fertile one, the procedure takes its toll. You feel like your fertility should be able to compensate for your lover's problems. Getting pregnant with the help of doctors divorces it from sex and love: it becomes a medical exercise. You feel like you've somehow failed at love, and you start questioning yourself and whether you want it as much as your partner. Is there something psychological standing in the way of conception? Is there some basic chemical incompatibility between us?

24 June 2007
Started the first round of IUI this week. I've been injecting myself for the past six days. It's not much fun, but I'm okay at it. I'm tired because I have had to be at the clinic early on both weekend days. My scan this morning showed that I had two follicles! Apparently my oestrogen wasn't great, though. More blood tests every day this week.

28 June 2007
Insemination day today. I am nervous and excited. Hardly slept last night, though, so am worried that will have a negative impact. Matt had a cold and snored half the night.

29 June 2007
Insemination was fine. Didn't like the stirrups. Was uncomfortable, like a bad smear, but not too bad. Twelve million sperm inserted. Had cramps last night but okay now. Bad timing as I have a huge deadline this week and Mai away from today. I am exhausted and have to work all weekend.

15 July 2007
Today is day five of my period. Round one of IUI did not work and I am gutted. Had counselling session on Friday. It was okay. It reinforced the need for Matt and I to stay solid as a couple.

27 July 2007
Awful week. When I finally finished work at 11 pm on Monday night I couldn't sleep. Resolved to resign. I had a very heated discussion on Tuesday morning with Mai, which cleared the air. Got home from work at 1 am. Insemination was the next day. It's so unfair that insemination day ended up being scheduled during one of the most stressful days of my working life. When I went to the bathroom just before I left to go to the clinic, I discovered I was bleeding. Had to have a scan and cervical examination and the doctor said the bleeding meant there was almost no chance of the procedure working. They had already prepared the sperm, so decided to go ahead because there would be no harm to me, but the message I got was that it was pretty pointless. Cried during insemination.

9 August 2007
I have a rotten cold, bad period pain, and found out yesterday that I need more surgery. Hysteroscopy now. It's never-ending. I'm angry with Matt for being out tonight when I need some comfort.

The purpose of the hysteroscopy was to check for polyps in Lecretia's uterus, which might have explained her irregular bleeding. But it turned up nothing unusual. Our spirits improved. We felt better about going into our third round of IUI, but it failed too. Each pregnancy test remained agonisingly absent of blue lines, a blank space on an impersonal plastic oracle.

> 3 November 2007
> I quit my job on Monday. Still can't quite believe it. Mai took it well. She offered for me to work part time, or take less responsibility. It made it hard. She is making moves to promote Catherine and Nick now, which was predictable, but quite gutting all the same. I'm annoyed with myself for being so sad about leaving. I think Matt was expecting me to come home and celebrate, but I just came home and cried. I have poured my heart and soul into that job and despite everything I feel very sad about leaving. I have barely slept for a month. I am so confused about what to do next. Andrew Butler of Russell McVeagh wants me to work for him, which is very flattering. But so does Geoffrey Palmer.

A few weeks earlier I had bumped into Sir Geoffrey at an event at the Opera House, and we spoke about Lecretia in depth. I told him of the pressure she was under, and how the long hours she was putting in at Chen Palmer were making her very unhappy.

'You've got to get her out of there,' I said, as though asking a firefighter to rescue someone from a burning building.

Lecretia resigned from Chen Palmer not because she disliked the work, but because having identified work as a contributor to her stresses she felt it was best to move on to somewhere with more manageable hours. Ultimately she decided to follow her old boss Sir Geoffrey Palmer to the Law Commission, where Geoffrey was the chief commissioner and she was appointed senior legal and policy adviser.

After Lecretia left, Mai offered Catherine Marks a promotion to principal, but Catherine wasn't interested in staying on at Chen Palmer without Lecretia. Catherine also resigned and took a job working with Andrew Butler and Tim Clarke at Russell McVeagh.

Chapter 7

AFTER FAILING THREE IUI cycles, we were now eligible for IVF. Though it's now a common medical intervention, IVF is still somewhat magical. Over the course of a couple of months, a woman is given a series of drugs to stimulate egg growth, and to delay slightly the release of those eggs so that they grow to the right size. At the correct point in time, the patient comes into the clinic and is strapped into a chair, her legs spread indelicately apart. A nurse rubs her belly with conductive jelly and moves an infra-red scanner over it, which broadcasts images to a monitor. The scanner is manipulated until the ovary comes into view.

The fertility doctor inserts a syringe into the ovary via the vagina and uterus. You can see the passage of the needle on the monitor. Once inside the ovary, the end of the needle seeks out egg follicles, which appear as small black disks, full of mystery and possibility. The doctor sucks the content of the first follicle out through the needle, and the small black disk shrinks into nothing. The procedure is repeated until all the follicles have been emptied. Then the eggs are taken away and mingled with the partner's sperm in a petri dish.

Numbers are very important in this world. The follicles are measured before they are sucked dry. Anything over fourteen millimetres in diameter is promising, and the more eggs that are harvested, the more chances of success.

Lecretia's ovaries were not producing eggs of the number and quality you would expect for someone of her age. Neither of these problems was insurmountable, but it was another blow in the ongoing struggle to conceive.

24 January 2008

Well, here I am in the middle of a round of IVF. I haven't felt like writing. I'm doing okay and staying positive. I'm feeling a bit unsupported, but hopefully Matt will remedy that. I am very tired. I made the choice to go to the Law Commission and put family first. It's going well. No stress. I found an IVF forum. It's interesting to read about other people's experiences. Makes me realise there are others who've had an even rougher time than I have. Despite the challenges I've faced, I am so thankful for everything I have. I am so lucky.

This was Lecretia's last diary entry. After finding her online forum, where women talked and shared their struggles to conceive, she focused her attention on others. She began to talk about her new online friends by their noms de plume, and I came to learn how others shared the struggles. It helped me too, I suppose.

After that first IVF round, in February 2008, we spent three anxious days waiting to hear whether any of the eggs had made it to blastocyst stage. What the embryologists hope to see is a fertilised egg, divided neatly into eight evenly sized cells within its thick outer lining. A blastocyst looks strange, like a cluster of bubbles.

At the end of our first cycle, we had two blastocysts. We had the first embryo implanted, and the second frozen.

It was unsuccessful.

After a few months, the second embryo was thawed, and implanted.

It was unsuccessful.

It was June before we could try again, but when we did, Lecretia had her best cycle so far. Eleven eggs were produced. We were over the moon. But only two made it to blastocyst stage. This time both were implanted.

Lecretia got pregnant.

We had wanted this for so long. Now we had it, there was a strange sense of disorientation. We were pregnant, and we were shocked. Suddenly all of the concerns of the past two years were replaced with new concerns. Is it healthy? Boy or girl? Where will it sleep? What will we call it? Do we need to buy a new car? A new house? Who do we tell? When do we tell them?

Lecretia and I bought a book of baby names, and I remember sitting in bed with her on a Saturday morning, reading out names. Though she was still weeks away from showing, her hand rested tenderly on her belly, as if the developing embryo could feel her gentle touch.

In her second month, Lecretia's mood began to change and she developed a larger appetite. She was a lot more irritable towards me, but this was mitigated by a general aura of purpose and contentment. The thing that she wanted most in life was happening, and the future seemed clear and full of hope.

Just before eight weeks, we went for a scan. When the ultrasound device was placed on Lecretia's belly, a picture of the developing child came into view, and there was the flicker of a beating heart, the slightest pulse of life. Lecretia's relief and her joy were glorious. 'Matt, we're having a baby!'

The standard advice is that you start informing people at twelve weeks, but now we began telling our closest friends and family. There were many congratulations—the people we shared this with knew how much Lecretia and I had struggled, and what she had gone through.

We were scheduled for a ten-week scan, and we drove to that appointment in trepidation, tempered with optimism. The clinic was in a leafy suburb. We sat down in its spacious waiting room, the minutes and seconds ticking by with the cadence of a heartbeat, until we were called into the obstetrician's examination room.

The woman we met was dispassionate and immune to our excitement. Lecretia got up on the bed in preparation for the scan and the consultant rubbed her belly with conductive jelly, and rested the scanner on it. Within a few moments, the image of the child appeared on the monitor, only slightly larger, and only slightly more distinct.

'There's the foetus,' she said. She manipulated the scanner and the image, searching. 'I can't see a heartbeat yet,' she said, 'but sometimes it can be tough to locate at this early stage.'

The next few minutes passed in absolute silence. Lecretia must have been in unbearable suspense—the arc of her life, and the beginning of her child's, rested in the touch of the scanner against her belly.

The doctor moved the device around Lecretia's belly for another five minutes, seeking the correct angle. The image remained very still.

'I'm sorry,' she said. She withdrew the scanner, and the image on the monitor flickered out of view, leaving only blackness.

Without a word, Lecretia pulled her top back down over her belly. She walked over and sat beside me, and we faced the obstetrician.

'I estimate that the foetus expired somewhere in the eighth week,' she said. 'Given its size and your complications, we'll need to schedule a D&C.'

A dilatation and curettage is a medical procedure for managing miscarriages or, less commonly, abortions. It's unpleasant, involving the scraping and scooping of the uterus to remove the foetal tissue. Lecretia burst into tears. For weeks, she had been imagining and picturing this growing baby, investing into it so much hope and love, fantasising about its birth and its childhood and its future, daydreaming about picking out its clothes, holding it close to her, feeding it, loving it. Now the fate of this tiny kernel was to be extracted by stainless steel and discarded.

When we got home, we held each other and wept. I tried to console her, but there was nothing I could say. We grieved for a future which had been so close to becoming ours, taken from us in a few short hours. We were back to being the infertile couple, the childless ones. I sent an email to our close friends, giving them the bad news, and added:

> I hope that you will remain discreet about this: we'd rather this news didn't spread any wider than it has to. And if you should cross paths with Lecretia in the coming weeks and months, I would personally appreciate it if you could treat her with the appropriate level of sensitivity.

> We will do our best to continue on and try again. You'll forgive us if you are not informed too early on should we meet with any success in the future. I do not want to have to send an email like this out ever again.

A couple of days after the miscarriage, I was lying in bed with Lecretia. Her lips were moving very slightly. Sometimes she did this when she was intently thinking about something, as though she were rehearsing a conversation.

'I'm sorry I've done this to you,' she said, suddenly.

'Done what?'

'You married a dud wife.'

'Darling, you're perfect. I don't want to be with anyone else.'

'But I can't give you children.'

'Children are only part of this for me. It's about being with you. That's all I want. If we can have children, great. If we can't, we'll deal with that too. But whatever happens, we'll be together. That's all we need—we have enough to be happy. It doesn't feel that way now, but we still have a future.'

'You would have a better future without me.'

'That's not true. There is no future I want that doesn't have you in it.'

She fell back into silence, but I could sense that she was thinking.

'If you want to leave me, I'll give you half of everything,' she said. 'You can move out. I'll give you money. You could start a new life and meet someone else. You could still have a family. I want you to be able to have children. It doesn't seem right that I'm stopping you from doing that.'

She seemed serious. In my mind's eye, I could see a long corridor with a light at the end. Every door along its length burst open, and through each I could see other possibilities, away from here, free of fertility treatments and free of New Zealand, free of despair. I could walk through any of these doors with a few simple, heartbreaking words. Lecretia had put me at the threshold of a life alone, a life different from this, and possibly better, but a life without her.

I opened my eyes.

'No,' I said, and every door but one slammed shut again, as quickly as they had opened. 'No matter what happens, Lecretia, I want to be with you.'

Chapter 8

WE RESUMED OUR IVF treatments again at the fertility clinic, but now we had exhausted our publicly funded options, and would need to pay the costs ourselves. A cycle of IVF, with all the procedures and monitoring and storage and tests and drugs, costs a little over $10,000, a sum that we could manage, just, through our savings and thrifty living. There was nothing else that we wanted to spend our money on.

In March 2009 we began our third cycle, the miscarriage still a raw and painful memory. But we found hope and resumed the vitamins and healthy living that seemed to have helped last time. Lecretia only produced seven viable eggs, four fewer than the previous cycle. Still, two of those were fertilised and two were transferred.

The tests were negative at the end of the month. She did not become pregnant.

Lecretia didn't let these trials affect her professional life, though, putting them to one side when she was at work. She was enjoying her role at the Law Commission. She had already completed, under Geoffrey Palmer's direction, a review of the War Pensions Act, recommending to government a fairer deal for New Zealand's veterans. She visited the Ohakea air force base and was taken up in an Iroquois helicopter, whose pilot decided that the seduction of her shriek was such that he executed a series of evasive manoeuvres to elicit more of them.

One day she visited the attorney-general, Christopher Finlayson, in his office at the parliament buildings with Geoffrey. Mr Finlayson is a fearsomely intelligent man, and fastidiously tidy. His office, by all accounts, is immaculate. When you enter parliament you're asked to wear a sticker that indicates whether you're a visitor, a tourist, or from the press. Lecretia sat in front of Mr Finlayson's mahogany desk and listened as Geoffrey and the attorney-general discussed points of law.

Lecretia's sticker came loose from her suit jacket, and cartwheeled through the air, landing sticky side down on the desk. Neither Geoffrey nor the attorney-general noticed, as they were deep in conversation, but Lecretia was horrified. She went to retrieve the sticker, but when she went to pull it away from the desk, it remained resolutely stuck to the varnished surface. In panic she used her fingernail to dislodge it, hidden behind her forearm, but it would not come free.

Geoffrey stood to leave, and Lecretia could only follow. She shook hands with the attorney-general and departed with Geoffrey, mortified that she'd left evidence of her visit.

In 2009 Lecretia began work on the Sale of Liquor Act, reviewing the laws in New Zealand that specify how alcohol is marketed and sold. She liaised with people representing hospitality groups, liquor companies, emergency services and addiction groups. Her chief discovery, after looking at the evidence from other countries and New Zealand, was the huge social and economic harm caused by alcohol consumption, and that the most effective tools the government had at its disposal for dealing with that harm were reducing opening hours and increasing taxes. She knew these weren't popular recommendations, but the evidence was clear, and she was convinced. As part of her research she accompanied Geoffrey on a ride-along with emergency services on Friday night in Courtenay Place, Wellington's central party zone, where we had first met.

They were joined by Cate Brett, an impressive and intelligent journalist and editor who was brought on board to balance their legal horsepower with her enviable media savvy. Lecretia and Cate took an instant liking to each other and became firm friends.

With her new working hours, Lecretia and I had time to cook and eat together, to go out and to keep the flame of our love kindled. We travelled to Abel Tasman National Park, and I took some of my favourite photos of her there, on one of the deserted beaches at sunset. We kayaked around the coast together. She sought out dancing lessons and cooking classes for us.

Lecretia was also regularly going to the gym, and she was becoming very fit. She did aerobics classes and weights and had a personal trainer who helped her with her regimen and advised her on nutrition.

In the middle of that year, we began our fourth cycle. This time there were six eggs, one less than the previous month. Again, two eggs were fertilised and implanted, one slightly more promising-looking than the other.

Lecretia got pregnant. We were filled with hope again, but this time we remained wary. Before we'd even had time for a scan, the foetus was declared unviable and we prepared ourselves for a second miscarriage. The fertility doctors wanted to perform a biopsy on the foetus, to learn more about why Lecretia's pregnancies weren't coming to term. She was dispensed drugs to bring on the release of the foetus, and she took these at home with me. We were given instructions to collect the foetus and bring it to the clinic.

The experience was awful. After taking the drugs, Lecretia complained of pains in her abdomen and pelvis, cramps and aches, and she felt nauseous. While she sat in the bathroom I crouched beside her with a flimsy purple ice cream container. After some time, a pinky-red-brown mass was expelled from her, while she wept and pushed her palm against the wall for support. We were confused and frightened and not completely confident that what we'd collected was the foetus that had caused Lecretia so much agony. But I transferred it to the medical container we'd been given and took it to the clinic. For all that effort, the tests didn't turn up anything unusual. It was just a standard unviable pregnancy, with no chromosomal abnormalities. We had hardened ourselves to this possibility, but it still hurt. Our window of opportunity was closing. Lecretia was thirty-seven, an age where our chances of getting pregnant were becoming ever smaller.

After the second failed pregnancy, I decided I wanted a change of scene on the work front too. I was doing well at the web design agency I was working at, but a couple of my colleagues had left to join a company called Xero, an online accounting software start-up based in Wellington. It was still early days, but the company had audaciously gone public in 2007, barely a year after it was formed. I was interviewed and hired, joining them as a business analyst in September 2009.

Just before Christmas that year, Lecretia was working in her office when she suffered a fall. She broke her left wrist and had to wear a cast. It was my first experience of having Lecretia somewhat dependent on me. She required help putting on a bra and dressing, and I needed to do all of the housework and chores. It wasn't a problem, though Lecretia's high standards meant that certain tasks had to be redone and some cooking thrown out.

Lecretia hated being dependent. It was against her character. She was a doer and a perfectionist. I rarely complained about caring for her, and she rarely complained about my help, but her frustration was clear. She wanted to get back to the gym so she could keep fit for our next cycle, but she compensated with various floor exercises.

Once her wrist had healed, we had our fifth cycle of IVF in early 2010. This time, there were five eggs, one fewer than last time, but again, two embryos were fertilised and implanted. Again, the two-week wait, and again, the results were negative.

Lecretia quietly reported her progress to her online community. We were getting used to negative results. Each setback remained heartbreaking, but we'd agreed, almost without talking about it, that there was still a lot of good in our lives, and that whatever the future held for us, we would stay happy.

Chapter 9

WE PLANNED A trip to Europe, to visit Lecretia's friends and her brother Jeremy in London. It would be the first time Lecretia had returned to Europe since she had worked there, and the first time we would travel there together. We decided to go to Italy and then to Spain, meeting Jeremy and his wife, Kate, in Andalusia, which we would explore together.

Lecretia's legal expertise had been achieving notice in Wellington circles. When the incumbent counsel was planning to step down as the justice adviser at the Department of the Prime Minister and Cabinet, Geoffrey wanted to put Lecretia's name forward as a candidate for a three-month secondment into the office. It was Lecretia's dream job: operating at the centre of power and making full use of her legal skills to advise the government of the day. The thought of it terrified her, but before heading off overseas she agreed to let Geoffrey put her name forward for the role.

After a brief stay in London, we travelled to Rome, and Lecretia delighted in showing me what she described as her favourite city. She took me to the Trevi Fountain, the Forum, the Pantheon, and the Galleria Borghese, and we braved the crowds at the Vatican to see the Sistine Chapel. I was overcome with the beauty of the place.

The scale of the Vatican forces you to think about divinity. It is either the truth, or the biggest compounding of lies in all of history. What I sensed was not holiness or grace, but more its opposite: the idea that nothing is real and everything is permitted, that the world is made up of storytellers and listeners, and that stories are the most powerful force in the universe. They can intertwine with one another, becoming stronger, creating patterns and motifs that become part of traditions or belief systems until truth is indistinguishable from fiction. Stories can compel people to go to war, to act against their interests, to sacrifice themselves, to hate or to love others, or to justify unspeakable acts in the name of good. Each of us is like a thread woven into that tapestry of stories and the Vatican is like a giant knot through which millions of threads run. Though those threads might be spun from lies and fiction, there is no denying that the knot exists, warping the fabric for all of us.

We visited friends in Turin, and were invited to a family lunch outside of the city. We ate outdoors in the sun at a long table under a shady tree. They served us local dishes, including *carne cruda*, which is minced meat, served blood-red and raw, seasoned with lemon and garlic. I was also brave enough to try tripe with tomato.

From there we spent a few days on the coast of the Ligurian Sea in Levanto, before exploring the Cinque Terre. From Corniglia, the third of the five villages, you can look out across the blue Ligurian water, but it is impossible to tell where the sea ends and the sky begins. Then we went north to Florence, and stayed at an apartment a few blocks from the Duomo. I was reading Vasari's *Lives of the Artists*, and instantly fell in love with Florence in a way that I hadn't with Rome.

One morning, Lecretia prepared for her Skype interview for the position in the Department of the Prime Minister and Cabinet. I set her up on our laptop and she spoke directly to her tribunal of interviewers. I wasn't present for the conversation, but I returned after an hour at the small museum at Dante Alighieri's birthplace.

'How did it go?'

'I don't know,' Lecretia said. 'But now I really want the job.'

'You'll get it,' I said. 'You're perfect for it.'

'I don't have the experience.'

'I've never seen you fail at work, darling. You're an amazing lawyer.'

'But this is a much bigger role—I'm not sure I'm ready.'

'No one is ever ready to take a step like that the first time. It's a choice. Step up and give it your best shot, or someone else will.'

'Well, there's no guarantee I'll get it.'

'No, but I believe in you.'

Soon after that we found out that Lecretia had been appointed, and she would begin as soon as she returned from holiday. She was thrilled. We celebrated by wandering through Florence, enjoying the paintings in the Uffizi Gallery and crossing the Ponte Vecchio. We had lunch in a little wine cellar, and bravely ordered bruschetta with lard and honey, which turned out to be absolutely delicious.

With Italy behind us, we travelled to Spain, and Lecretia loved luxuriating on the broad and sandy Barcelona beaches. We explored the Sagrada Família, Gaudí's famous cathedral-in-progress. We made a promise to return one day, when it was finished, in 2026. We then travelled to Granada to meet with Jeremy and Kate. We visited the Alhambra and sampled the tapas bars. We went to the steaming public baths at Hammam Al Ándalus.

In Seville, we wandered around the labyrinthine streets. Lecretia really struggled with them. I often walked faster than her and would find myself charging ahead, then having to turn back to wait for her to catch up. There were moments when she would stand still, looking around for directions, waiting for me to come and rescue her.

Was this the first sign something was wrong? It is hard to know—I had always been the navigator. We didn't encounter the same problems in Córdoba or Ronda or Málaga, but she would stop and ask where we were, sometimes, prompting me to pull out my map and check we were still on track.

We returned to New Zealand, and her new job, in July 2010. She threw herself into it, informing me after the first day that she'd had a security briefing and that she couldn't share any parliamentary business with anyone, even me. But I know how much she enjoyed those three months, and how well she performed. In October 2010, the chief executive of the DPMC, Maarten Wevers, sent a letter to Geoffrey at the Law Commission praising her performance, singling out her contribution to a range of urgent legal issues arising from the Canterbury earthquake, a contribution for which he said he was especially thankful. 'If we were ever to need someone in future for a similar assignment,' he added, 'I'm sure Lecretia would be on our list of persons to approach.'

Lecretia returned to the Law Commission, but set a goal of returning to the DPMC one day in the role that she'd held for a few short months. And the door was open to her to do that. She'd seen her future.

We resumed our lives, and elected to opt for one more round of IVF. In this cycle there were only four eggs, and only one was fertilised. It didn't look great, but it was implanted, and it didn't take. Her doctors were no closer to knowing why. Though there was nothing wrong with the blastocysts, they just wouldn't develop into pregnancies. After exhausting all other possibilities, the doctors decided that Lecretia's eggs must be the problem and that our best chance was to search for a donor.

While contemplating this, Lecretia took up classes in cake decoration. She was learning how to craft flowers out of sugar. She used to bring her creations home: delicate roses, tulips, leaves and more. I hadn't seen this artistic side of her before. I think it brought her happiness to be creating something simple, with her hands, that was beautiful and small and sweet.

One night, driving home alone from a class, she ran into trouble. The weather was terrible, and as she approached a slight bend, she hit a parked car on her left, writing off her car and doing a lot of damage to the other. She walked away shaken but unharmed.

A nearby resident took her into his house to look after her while the tow truck arrived. There had been accidents before on the bend, he said. I taxied out and picked her up, while our car was towed away. After that, Lecretia encouraged me to do more of the driving, too scared to get behind the wheel herself.

Christmas in 2010 was to be at Debra's again. I drove us up to Auckland on Christmas Day. It was a beautiful day, and Debra had set up tables outside, on her driveway, with a marquee. It was almost like a wedding reception. We had a glorious day with Lecretia's aunts and uncles.

As we left in the afternoon and walked out to the car, Lecretia did something strange. She walked past our car, and opened the door of the one behind it, another white car, which happened to be unlocked. Then she sat in the passenger seat, staring at me, as if to say, 'What are you waiting for?'

'That's not our car, Lecretia!' I said.

She was momentarily confused, until she realised that she was indeed in the wrong vehicle. She got out and we laughed about it, but mixed with her laughter, I can remember now, was embarrassment and confusion.

Shortly after Christmas, while spending a few days at her parents' home in Tauranga, Lecretia started to talk to her mother about the fact she was getting headaches. She'd spoken to her GP about them, and been prescribed pain relief, but it hadn't worked all that well. After talking to Shirley, she resolved to get a referral to see a neurologist, just in case.

When she got home, Lecretia and I discussed the next steps in having a child. We talked about possible donors. I had my preferred donors and she had hers. We agonised over who to approach and how to ask them. It is illegal in New Zealand to pay someone to be a donor for you, but there are certain US states where you can. Lecretia investigated this process, and became convinced that it was the right choice for us. She chose a clinic in San Diego.

Lecretia would have been a wonderful mother. She was so caring and generous and kind, and had so much warmth and heart. Like her, I wanted our love to be expressed through children. But I was obsessed with the idea that the child should be fully ours. Lecretia was special, and her children would be special. A child born from a donor egg would be hers, but it wouldn't be *like* her, wouldn't share her beauty, or her spirit—and that was what I wanted. It seemed so petty, but I couldn't get past it. Was I being selfish? Did I love my wife too much? Did I not love her enough?

I took a lot of convincing. I felt that if the child was not biologically hers I would have to choose to love it. But for her there was no such doubt—her desire to be a mother was the source of her love. A child to call her own, no matter its origins, would be like a vessel that desire would flow into, allowing it full expression, transforming it into a mother's love.

I did not have the same boundless compulsion to be a father—I did not want a child at any cost. But when I focused on Lecretia's desire to be a mother, and what having a child would mean to her, I gave my consent. I had my love for her, and that was what I drew upon. I wanted more than anything for her to be a mother, because that was what she wanted, and she deserved it more than anyone.

Meanwhile she'd been to see her GP, and got a referral for a neurology appointment in a few months' time. She pushed for something earlier but there was nothing available. She was still taking migraine medication. While Lecretia endured her headaches, we looked at possible donors, and settled on a young woman we both liked. We weren't given many details, but knew that she came from a family of Iraqi refugees, and something about her in her photos reminded us of Lecretia.

As we organised San Diego, Lecretia became more and more excited. She believed that her eggs were the fundamental problem. Now we had a donor she was filled with hope.

One morning, walking to work, taking the same route through the botanical gardens that she always took, Lecretia called me. 'Matt, they've moved the lamppost.'

'What do you mean?'

'It's not where it was. They've moved it over to another part of the garden and put it in a stupid place.'

'That's a shame,' I said. 'They must have had a reason.'

'It doesn't make any sense where it is now.'

'Things change, I guess.'

'I don't like it,' she said. 'It's not the same any more. Why do things have to change?'

Chapter 10

LECRETIA'S GP CALLED in February 2011 to tell us that she'd managed to secure an earlier neurology appointment. We agreed to go to the appointment before booking our flights to San Diego.

In the last two months Lecretia's headaches had worsened. She described her vision as 'crazy' but had trouble describing it in any further detail.

Lecretia was nervous about the appointment, and so was I. Neither of us dared to utter what we feared the most. We met with Dr David Abernethy, a respected neurologist, late on a Monday afternoon at his office at Wakefield Hospital in Newtown. It was in a large examining room a few floors up in a building that was dim and quiet with dark-stained wooden interiors. Dr Abernethy was a stern man, but I felt I was in the presence of someone who knew his field and was trustworthy.

Dr Abernethy began to examine Lecretia. He checked her sight, her perception of colour, sound and movement, and her reflexes. He performed basic tests: *squeeze my hands, lift your right arm and now your left*. He held up his finger and moved it around Lecretia's field of vision, mapping out its extremities. Something was wrong. Lecretia could not see anything on the left-hand side of her body.

If you look straight ahead and imagine everything left of your nose missing from your field of view, that was Lecretia's experience. But she hadn't realised it. Her brain was tricking her into thinking she was seeing a full picture.

That something so glaringly wrong had escaped my notice was crushing. How could such a fundamental problem not be obvious? How had I missed it?

Dr Abernethy scheduled urgent scans for the next day. He expected some sort of abnormality. He told us that much. We left his office in shock.

I rang Shirley: 'We saw the neurologist. Something's wrong and we're not sure what. Lecretia's getting scans tomorrow. You'd better get down here.'

Did we sleep that night? I don't remember. Did we cry? We must have. Lecretia had her MRI the next day at 2 pm. I was invited into the room but had to stay behind a curtain. I could not see what was going on, but I could listen. All I could hear was the clank and whirr of a mysterious machine. I wondered what the radiologists were seeing. Something was wrong with my wife.

Dr Abernethy told us afterwards we should see him at Wellington Hospital first thing the next morning. He told us that there was something on the scan and that we needed to see it.

We arrived early. The suspense of the situation affected us in different ways. Lecretia was quiet and calm, as though numb. I was full of adrenalin and felt like the smallest thing could send me into a panic. The receptionist told us Dr Abernethy hadn't arrived yet. She answered us in a weary but firm voice. We sat and waited. Some other people had brought along books. I wondered what they were here for. There was music—Peter Cetera was singing 'If You Leave Me Now'. I held Lecretia's hand and she rested her head on my shoulder. My other hand drummed incessantly on the arm of the chair beside me. My mind was racing. We didn't speak.

We saw Dr Abernethy arrive and walk through the reception area, pulling a wheeled suitcase behind him. He was twenty minutes late. If he saw us he didn't acknowledge us. He disappeared somewhere behind reception.

As we waited, I listened to the receptionists arguing about how to restructure his appointments to adjust for the late start. 'Don't move Imogen,' one of them said. 'She's the really sick one.'

Dr Abernethy appeared and called Lecretia's name. He took us to a small room off the main corridor and offered us both a seat.

He told us he hadn't actually seen the scans yet, but that he had been informed there was something on them. As he loaded them onto the computer he warned us that whatever we saw might be subtle. The first few images showed nothing. But then a white shape appeared, and swelled like burnt celluloid until we came to rest on an image of the entire thing—a fat white mass that covered a quarter of her brain, and pushed hard against the brain's centre.

It was not subtle. Lecretia didn't want to look at it, and I couldn't blame her.

If she'd complained earlier, a little more, a little harder, we might have taken her to the emergency department. They might have noticed something when examining her, booked a scan, and we would have been looking at something less grotesque. In this room, she and I realised that her stoicism might have cost us her life, and that it was her insistence on seeing a neurologist urgently that might now have saved it.

'Okay,' said Dr Abernethy. 'This is very serious.'

'What is it?' I said.

'Until we take a biopsy we won't know for sure. But it is almost certainly a glioma.'

'Cancer?'

'Yes. I'm sorry.'

As he looked at the scans again, I put my arm around Lecretia and squeezed her shoulder. She absorbed the news in silence. There was a strange dissonance in having my arm around this woman and at the same time seeing the contents of her skull displayed in slices on a black-and-white screen.

'I'm going to book you in to see a neurosurgeon tomorrow. I'm almost certain he'll have to operate. If you look at this scan, you can see how the left side of the brain is causing something called midline shift, and it's compressing the brain stem.'

I could see what he meant. One half of the brain dwarfed the other, and the midline had bulged out towards the other hemisphere, squashing the central cavity.

I started asking Dr Abernethy questions, and he answered as best he could. 'The neurosurgeon will be able to tell you more,' he said finally. 'Take some time to process this news. I suspect you'll be dealing with this situation for a while: this is just the beginning. You'll have plenty of time for questions.'

We left. Lecretia remained silent.

'Do you want to get a coffee?' I asked uselessly. She didn't drink coffee.

'I just want to go home.'

Once we were in the car and driving she let herself go. As I turned out of the hospital we both started to cry. I wiped my eyes and drove on. I probably shouldn't have been driving. But my girl wanted to go home, and I wanted to do whatever she wanted. I couldn't fathom the impact it must have had on her. We were so close to going to San Diego. So close to starting our family. We knew that everything had changed and the future that we thought we had together was now nothing more than a distant fantasy.

This woman, who had given me so much, shown me so much love, needed me now more than ever. I resolved, on that journey home, to do everything I could to help her.

Once I'd got Lecretia home, Shirley arrived from Tauranga, and she took her daughter in her arms and they both burst into tears.

'I'm sorry, Mum,' Lecretia said, as though she were somehow to blame. 'I'm not going to be able to look after you like I promised.'

I decided I should talk to my boss and sent him a quick note, asking to see him to discuss something personal. He agreed to meet, and I went into the office to explain. He told me to go home and not to worry about work.

We received a call later that morning from a neuro-surgeon, Kelvin Woon, who made an appointment to see us that night. We drove back to the hospital for the second time.

Kelvin was younger than either of us. He was personable, but his voice had a sense of urgency.

'Lecretia,' he said. 'On the scans it looks very much like a glioma, which is a form of brain tumour. Until we operate, we won't know for certain. There are many different types of brain tumour.'

The news was hard to comprehend. Was she dying or not? How much time did we have? Kelvin pulled up the scans.

'Do you see here how the mass of the tumour is pressing on the centre line of the brain? That's a big problem. If we don't treat the tumour, it will cut off circulation of fluids around the brain stem, which regulates your body's vital functions—your muscles, your breathing, your nervous system. If we do nothing, you will probably enter a coma from which you will not wake up.'

'How long until that happens?' asked Lecretia.

'It's hard to say, but based on the size of the tumour and the way it appears to be growing, it could be within weeks.'

How was it possible that my wife, walking around, talking, doing her job and laughing and smiling, could end up in a coma within weeks? Could things really move that quickly? The room felt cold.

'So what do we do?' I asked.

'We need to operate. We will cut open Lecretia's skull, and where it's safe to do so, I will remove the tumour. Whatever we remove will be submitted for biopsy, so we know how best to treat the tumour after that. We'll find out what grade the tumour is. To me it looks like an astrocytoma, which tends to be a lower-grade tumour and which may respond very well to additional treatments.'

'What does grade mean?'

'Tumours are graded from one to four. Grade one tumours are very slow growing. Grade four is the most aggressive. If it's grade one, you might have decades of life left. If it's grade four, then you might only have a few years, if that. But, like I said, it doesn't look like a grade four tumour. We'll find out with the biopsy.'

'Is it risky?' Lecretia asked.

'Yes. There is very small chance that you might not survive the surgery. And of course we are dealing with the brain, and we are removing some parts of the brain that are very important. The tumour is located near your occipital, temporal and parietal lobes. I've reviewed your notes about your vision problems, and your issues with short-term memory and navigation, so we know those things are already affected by the tumour. After surgery those symptoms are likely to become permanent. Also, the surgery could make you blind, or you could lose your sense of smell, or the ability to speak, or it could affect your memory, or it could do all of those things.'

It was an awful dilemma: risk a coma or even death, or risk the loss of things that made Lecretia who she was. Would she taste food again? Would she be able to see her family and friends? Would she recognise me, be able to talk to me? What if she came out of surgery and didn't know who I was?

'I'll take as few risks as possible,' Kelvin said. 'I'll remove as much of the tumour as I can, safely, and I think I'll be able to remove enough to reduce the pressure on the brain stem. But looking at the scan, it's very unlikely that I'll be able to remove it all. You'll almost certainly need further treatment afterwards.'

'Like what?' I asked.

'Radiotherapy, chemotherapy. But first of all we need to operate to remove the immediate danger.'

'I need time to think about it,' said Lecretia.

I was incredulous. 'What's to think about? You'll have the surgery, right?' I said.

'I just want to think it over and make sure I'm sure.'

'That's okay,' said Kelvin. 'Here's my number. Call me when you know what you want to do.'

That in itself was an indication of how serious things were. How bad do things need to be before a neurosurgeon will offer you his mobile number?

'Look,' said Kelvin. 'You need to stay positive and stay hopeful. There's an excellent chance that the surgery will be successful and that with treatment you'll have many more years of quality life. But we need to move quickly.'

We left the consulting room. Kelvin shook my hand as I left and I felt his compassion. I walked with Lecretia back to the car.

'How did we get here?' I asked on the drive home.

Lecretia didn't respond. She stared straight ahead, tears glistening on her cheeks. I cried too. Every visit to a doctor brought fresh tears. New revelations about Lecretia's condition and its consequences were being heaped upon us faster than we could deal with them.

At home, Lecretia changed into her pyjamas, her dressing gown, and her ugg boots. She sat on the bed and stared out the window, and cried in a way I'd never seen before. It was a lament. Until that day she had still been hopeful about San Diego, and starting a family, but now we would need to cancel those plans, almost certainly forever. I held her and didn't say a word. What was there to say?

After a while I let her go. I took her hands and held them. 'Whatever happens, I'm going to be right beside you, babe. I'll hold your hand through all of this. I'll take care of you, I promise.'

'I don't want to lose my sight. I don't want to not know who you are. I don't want any of that.'

'That probably won't happen. It won't happen. You're healthy and strong: there's no reason it won't go well.'

'You don't know that.'

'We have to think positive, babe. We have to. Are you seriously considering not having surgery?'

'I don't want to hold you back. I don't want you to have to look after me. Maybe it would be easier for everyone if I didn't have surgery.'

'Are you kidding? You have to do this. I'll look after you. If I don't do a good job, I'm sure your mother will help. I don't want to lose you. Lecretia, you're everything to me. I need you.'

Lecretia was clearly working through what all this might mean for others, and hadn't even started thinking about what it might mean for her. Her selflessness in this situation was a flaw. It was also a quintessentially Kiwi attitude: what would cause the least fuss, the least bother for everyone?

Like me, Shirley couldn't believe that Lecretia would even consider not having the surgery.

'Whatever happens, I'll look after you, Lecretia. Matt and I will be here for you.'

'You have work, Mum. I don't want you looking after me for years and years. Dad needs you.'

'If you need me, I'll look after you. You're my girl. You and Jeremy and Kat are the most important things in my life.'

'I don't want to make this difficult for anyone.'

Lecretia's instinctive kindness and consideration for others were overriding her instinct for self-preservation. But she was also afraid of what might happen to her. Her identity was bound up in her wellness and wholeness. Perhaps she already sensed she would have to reappraise who she was, and wasn't sure she could do it, or that she wanted to do it.

'You have to have the surgery,' I said. 'I need you, and your family needs you. You're too important to us.'

I'm not sure whether Lecretia was really entertaining the idea of not going ahead with her surgery, but framing it as something that we needed and wanted her to do seemed to help her accept that seeking surgery wasn't selfish, and that she could feel okay about doing it, and finally she agreed.

I called the neurosurgeon. 'Lecretia wants to have the surgery.'

'Good,' he said. 'It's the right decision. I've scheduled it for Wednesday next week. Lecretia should come to the neurological ward on Tuesday afternoon. We'll go from there.'

I talked to Lecretia about telling people and she agreed that we should. I emailed our friends with the news, and told them to come and visit Lecretia if they wanted to. It seemed important, since there was a risk she wouldn't survive the surgery.

The news people were expecting to hear was that we'd finally got pregnant, but this was entirely different. No one saw it coming or was quite sure how to take it. The most affected were Lecretia's family and the girls she'd grown up with.

To her family, she was the shining light. Her successes and kindness and beauty were a source of strength for everyone. To her friends, she was the gorgeous, glamorous one, the girl whose smile asserted itself in every photograph, whose humility and heart chased out all jealousy.

People started arriving in Wellington to see her. Lecretia seemed strengthened by these visits, which reminded her that she had so much to live for, and that so many people cared about her. Couriers knocked on our door, bearing gifts sent from London, Washington and

Dubai. Our visitors crowded in and sat on the floor, or out on our deck in the lingering summer sun. Lecretia laughed and smiled, and was delighted to see people, particularly those who had travelled great distances.

I became obsessed with photographing Lecretia— I sensed that after surgery, if she survived, and the ensuing radiotherapy, she would be changed, and I wanted as many images of her as I could get. We went up to the botanical gardens, near the top of Wellington's cable car, and I took dozens of photographs with the green and blue harbour and city behind her.

In truth, though, the photos taken over that weekend are not my favourites. She smiled and laughed and posed by herself and with her family, but the unmistakable tightness in her eyes and smile betrayed her private panic and pain. She was grateful for the love that was heaped upon her that weekend, but in moments alone with me she reached for me and let me take her in my arms and she wept.

The weekend culminated in a late lunch at a restaurant in town with her family. I sat beside Lecretia and she sat across from her parents. We talked about Christmases and nieces and nephews and the summer we'd all just enjoyed.

But there was a moment when her father, Larry, flung his hand out in front of him in a demonstrative gesture, and sent his glass of red wine flying. The wine arced out of the glass and hit Lecretia's white dress, spreading out quickly into a blood-red stain.

Larry was horrified at what he'd done. The heavy symbolism of the red wine on the elegant white dress was too much for him. His body quaked and he burst into tears.

'It's all right, Dad,' said Lecretia. 'It's just bad luck.'

On Monday night, Lecretia and I went to her favourite restaurant in Wellington, a bistro called Capitol. She looked glorious and I wondered if I would ever see her this way again. The sun poured into the restaurant through thin wooden blinds, bathing us in a golden light.

'I love you, sweetheart,' I said. 'I'm so sorry this is happening to you.'

'I'm scared, Matt,' she said.

'I'm scared too. But I know it'll be okay. It has to be. I need you.'

She extended her hand. I held it for a long time. Her slender fingers entwined with my own. Her hands were always cool to the touch, but within a few moments they were as warm as mine.

'I really thought we were going to have a family,' Lecretia said.

'We still might,' I said. 'When you beat this thing, we'll get back in touch with San Diego. We can pick up where we left off. There's no reason why we can't.'

'Maybe you should try with someone else.'

'Don't be silly. When I married you, I meant it. You're everything to me. Children or no children. That wasn't a condition of marrying you. There were no conditions. I wanted to be with you whatever the future held, even this. You changed my life.'

'I ruined your life.'

'You did not. I'm a better person because of you. If it weren't for you I'd still be eating pizza three nights a week. You're the best thing that ever happened to me.'

That night we made love, desperately, quietly, passionately, as though it might be the last time. Afterwards we held each other and slept that way until morning.

The next day, we went to Wellington Hospital.

Once she was settled in the neurological ward, she dug through her handbag and pulled out a greeting card in plastic wrapping. She unwrapped it, wrote a message and signed it. She handed it to me.

'This is a birthday card for Aunty Pat. Make sure you send it, okay?'

'Okay,' I said.

'Don't forget.'

I stayed with her that night in the hospital, sitting beside her while she struggled to sleep. I held her hand in the dark and we listened to the mysterious sounds of the hospital: the ceaseless beeping of machines, the footsteps of nurses in the corridors, the snoring and moans and cries of patients.

'It's going to be okay,' I said.

'I know. And if it isn't, I've had such a lovely weekend, Matt. I'm so lucky.'

We had lived the last few days as though they were Lecretia's last: with food and friends and family. We had done everything we could, and now it was up to the neurosurgeon, and fate, to take us through the looking glass. Lecretia was ready.

In the morning, Lecretia's family came to see her before she went into the operating theatre. She hugged and kissed everyone in turn and said a few words to each.

I walked beside Lecretia's bed as she was wheeled through the hospital. A set of double doors loomed ahead.

'Okay, this is as far as you can go,' the orderly told me.

'Matt, you have an eyelash,' said Lecretia.

I leaned over her, and her delicate fingers brushed my cheek.

'Got it,' she said, and smiled.

I kissed her one last time, and stood back, and the orderly pushed the bed forward through the doors. Lecretia's eyes met mine. And then the doors swung shut, leaving me alone.

Chapter 11

THE WAIT WAS unbearable. I spent most of it sitting in the hospital café, drinking bad coffee and answering emails.

Shortly after lunch I received a call from the neuro-surgeon.

'The surgery has been successful. We were able to de-bulk the tumour. Lecretia will be awake shortly.'

I felt a huge relief and went to find Lecretia. She was lying in bed, slightly elevated, with a bandage around her skull, but her eyes were open and clear. Dried blood bloomed purple beneath the outer layers of gauze where her skull had been pinned back together and her skin stapled up. The left side of her scalp had been shaved.

'How are you, babe?'

I didn't know what to expect. My poor wife had had her skull sawn open and parts of her brain removed. Would she recognise me? Know my name? Be able to speak?

'I'm sore,' she said, and smiled.

'Oh, babe,' I said.

I gingerly hugged her, careful not to move her, but grateful for the contact. It felt like she'd been on a long journey, one that had physically changed her. She was slow and measured in her movements but well aware of her surroundings. 'Did you send that birthday card to Aunty Pat?' she asked.

I sat with her that night and slept in the chair beside her bed while she dozed.

The next day she was moved to another room on the ward, which she shared with an older woman in her seventies.

Her friend Angela came to visit. Lecretia told her she was upset that they'd shaved only half her hair off. The hair that remained was matted with dried blood. Angela grabbed a pair of scissors and trimmed her remaining hair, then took a sponge and a bowl of water and mopped up the blood that had congealed around the staples holding her skull together.

Doctors came to visit and after twenty-four hours suggested Lecretia might like to try walking. As soon as they left, Lecretia asked me to help her out of bed so that she could try.

She stood and then rocked on her feet for a moment before taking a couple of steps. I took her arm and slowly walked with her out of the ward and up the corridor. We went thirty metres and came back again. She didn't lose her balance once.

The old lady next to Lecretia had suffered a stroke and was in her very final days. She could say only one or two words. She had very few visitors, and was lonely. On one occasion we watched as she rang the bell for the nurses repeatedly. I went out to the nurses' station. There was no one there. When I returned to the ward the old lady moaned and, clearly distressed, emptied her bowels into her bed, and the smell of it quickly filled the small room.

I finally found a nurse coming out of another ward and described the problem.

'Yes, we'll be right there.'

It took another fifteen minutes for the nurses to show up. They rolled the old lady onto her side and changed the sheets. They roughly wiped her bottom and told her how naughty she was. Every time they shifted her, the smell in the room grew stronger.

We felt so bad for that old lady. She had done nothing wrong—she was only dying. But she was at the mercy of her health, and the nurses she shared with all the other patients. She clearly prided herself on her appearance and looked after herself—her nails were manicured, her hair a tight perm—but sadly she'd found herself in the neurological ward of a public hospital, with few visitors and attended to by overworked and underpaid nurses who scurried from one minor crisis to another.

According to palliative care statistics, most of us will die in a hospital. If we've kept up our friendships and relationships we might have a few visitors. But at our most helpless we will likely be cared for by people who don't know us or love us. It's no surprise that most of us would rather not die there. A hospital is designed to save lives and to propel us back out into the world. It is not designed for living or dying.

Chapter 12

LECRETIA SPENT TWO more days in hospital. The surgery was successful. The tumour had been tamed, but not excised completely. A piece of it had been sent off to the lab for biopsy. The results would tell us what type of tumour Lecretia had.

Her condition improved steadily. She walked out of the front doors of the building unassisted, her head still bandaged. When we got home I held her arm as I walked her into the house down the narrow concrete path.

I had been off work for two weeks, and I was still finding my place at Xero. I was worried too that Lecretia might need to finish work for good, and that I would be financially responsible for looking after both of us. We had a mortgage and bills to pay and I didn't want Lecretia to feel that she had to go back to work before she was ready. So we agreed I would go back to work, and Shirley would take some time off to look after her.

Lecretia spent most of the following weeks sleeping at home, being nursed by her mother. Ferdinand would sit with her on the sofa or at the end of the bed. It was still warm and sunny in March but the sunlight hurt her eyes, so she spent a lot of time inside.

We returned to Lecretia's oncologist, who showed us the scans and gave us the results of the histology report. The suspicions were confirmed—Lecretia had a diffuse astrocytoma, with elements of oligodendroglioma.

A more serious tumour, like a glioblastoma, is shaped like a dense marble of tissue that slowly expands. This was more formless, as though someone had blown a puff of smoke into her ear. It meant it was hard for anything to get a grip on it—whether a scalpel, or a drug, or a particle beam. The cancer was growing along two cellular pathways: the astrocytes, which form the supportive tissue of the brain, and the oligodendrocytes, which perform a similar function. The cancer was attacking the structural glue holding Lecretia's brain together.

The tumour was still present. It stretched from the front to the back of her brain. It had crossed the central cortex and begun to take root in the right hemisphere. Lecretia's vision had not improved, which was to be expected, since the surgery had removed part of the brain responsible for visual function. It was extremely unlikely she would ever regain the left side of her field of vision.

The oncologist informed us that radiotherapy would begin in two weeks. The therapy targets the cancer cells, but it would kill healthy brain cells too. Because Lecretia's tumour was diffuse, this was inevitable. He also said that it was important, once we started, not to skip a day of treatment. The radiotherapy would be less effective if we missed any sessions.

The night before Lecretia started radiotherapy, we went out for dinner. She wore a skullcap and dressed up beautifully for the occasion. I held her hand across the table.

'I'm so sorry about all this,' I said.

'It's not your fault.'

'I feel helpless—I don't know what to do to help you.'

'You're doing it. You're here for me. But I thought we'd grow old together and I thought we'd have children. I really wanted children. That was my plan.'

'So what's your plan now?'

'I don't have one any more.'

*

The first session of radiotherapy was on the second floor of Wellington Hospital. We entered a room where a huge machine dwarfed everything else in it. The machine looked like something out of *2001: A Space Odyssey*, with huge off-white plastic panels and chunky curves.

Afterwards I asked her how it felt, and she said, 'It's like being inside a photocopier.'

After the first week we were informed the hospital would be closed on Good Friday and Easter Monday, so the radiotherapy would be suspended.

'But we were told that we couldn't skip a day of treatment—four days without treatment, isn't that bad?'

'It's not worth worrying about.'

The radiotherapy left Lecretia more and more fatigued. Light hurt her eyes and she was bothered by loud noises. She sat in silent contemplation like a nun, not in search of some revelation, but because the ordinary business of thinking and seeing was a source of acute pain.

After Easter, Shirley watched as they placed Lecretia in the machine. The nurse on duty was training a new staff member.

'You see these two red lines?' she said, indicating two red beams of light that formed a cross where the radiotherapy sequence would begin. 'You need to line the horizontal one up across the back of the skull here, and the vertical one up through the skull, and down the centre of the back and between the legs, so that it's nice and centred.'

'Okay,' said the trainee.

'Once you've got everything lined up correctly, you can begin.'

The next day, Lecretia and Shirley were surprised to see two different nurses on duty. Shirley watched as they placed her daughter in the radiotherapy machine. She could see that they had not correctly lined up the vertical red beam.

Out of earshot of Lecretia, she pulled the nurses aside and told them.

'It's fine,' insisted the nurse. 'Please leave the room now. We're about to begin.'

Shirley left, simmering with anger. When Lecretia emerged twenty minutes later, Shirley asked her how she was.

'I don't know, Mum,' she said, 'but it felt different today, like it was in the wrong place.'

At the next session with the oncologist, Shirley complained about what had happened.

'Why didn't you say something?' asked the oncologist.

'I did! They pushed me out of the room!' she replied.

The next day, however, when Lecretia returned to radiology, the original nurse was there and she pulled

Shirley aside. 'I'm so sorry,' she said. 'I was off that day. They got bureau people in who weren't trained. It'll be okay, I promise, but I'll make sure someone is there who's properly trained next time or they'll postpone the treatments. This doesn't normally happen.'

What we learned, in our experiences in the health system, is that 'what normally happens' is subject to unplanned absences, computer glitches, lost notes, failures to follow up, confusion about next steps, misunderstandings. Continuity of care was often quoted as an aspiration, but the system is run by busy people who have an appointment with someone else right after they have dealt with you. They are overworked and underpaid. The Kiwi mentality—don't make a fuss, don't cause trouble—can work against you, possibly even kill you. In a hospital, as in life, the squeaky wheel gets the oil.

Lecretia's last session of radiotherapy was in May, and she took a few days to recover.

'I have to get back to work,' she said.

'You've just had radiotherapy—you can take more time.'

'No, I can't,' she said. 'Now that the radiotherapy is done, I don't have any more excuses.'

She returned to the Law Commission on slightly reduced hours, finishing at 3 pm. Shirley and I tried to convince her that it wasn't necessary, but she was insistent. She felt that she should be there, putting the work in.

Her hair gradually fell out, leaving only scabs and redness. The tops of her ears and the side of her face were burnt and cracked. It was painful. I rubbed aloe vera into her scalp every night, but it offered only slight relief.

While this was going on I did a lot of reading about Lecretia's condition. I got *The Neurology Handbook* out of the Philson Library at the University of Auckland, and read up on her specific condition. Aside from PCV, an intravenous treatment that had been the standard of care since the eighties, the latest wonder drug was called temozolomide. It cost close to $2000 a month.

I also found a reference to an academic paper called 'Prognostic Factors for Survival in Adult Patients with Cerebral Low-Grade Glioma' by F. Pignatti et al. I found the paper online and devoured its contents. Lecretia's doctors had refused to offer any thoughts on a prognosis— saying Lecretia could have from a year to many decades of good health.

The paper talked about five factors that statistically predict mean survival times from diagnosis. They were whether the tumour was over six centimetres in diameter at any point, whether it had crossed the midline, the presence of any neurological deficit such as cognitive impairment or loss of vision, whether the person was over forty, and whether the tumour was made up of one type of brain cell or several. The fact that Lecretia was still under forty and that the tumour had more than one cell type both worked in her favour. At the bottom of the fourth-to-last page was a little table you could use to calculate a patient's likely survival time, which indicated that Lecretia had between 3.2 and 4.8 years. Statistically, around 95 per cent of patients in Lecretia's situation would live a little more than three years but less than five. From the date of her diagnosis, that worked out to be between June 2014 and December 2015. I never told Lecretia about this prognosis. After seeing it, and storing it away in my memory, I tried to put it out of my mind.

Shirley had done some reading of her own, and had seen some promising literature on intravenous vitamin C treatment. This is where you're hooked up to a drip which feeds you a superdose of vitamin C for a couple of hours. The treatment wasn't sanctioned by the hospital, but we were willing to try anything that might help, so Lecretia enrolled in a Wellington clinic out in Newtown, where she ingested the vitamin for an hour or two a couple of afternoons a week.

After a couple of weeks of treatment, I got a call from the clinic.

'I'm afraid there's been an incident with Lecretia. She collapsed in the bathroom and fell to the floor, hitting her head. She's been taken by an ambulance to the emergency department at Wellington Hospital.'

'What happened?'

'We're not sure. We found her on the floor of the bathroom. She'd been unconscious for a while. But she's on her way to the hospital now.'

I raced to the emergency department to be with her. On the way I called Larry and Shirley, who had both returned home to Tauranga, and told them what had happened. They booked flights at once.

In the emergency department I found Lecretia sitting up in bed. She turned to me as I entered the room.

'Hello,' she said, groggily.

'What happened?'

'I think I fell,' she said. She was blinking slowly and looked unsteady.

A doctor arrived to examine her. The doctor was brisk and efficient. He looked at her and examined her and asked her how she was doing.

'Do you think you might have had a seizure?' he asked.

'I don't know,' she said.

'Are you on any anti-seizure medication?'

She looked confused.

'No,' I said, and I rattled off the drugs that I knew she was taking.

And then, as if on cue, her eyes closed and her hands rose in front of her and her mouth opened and her head flew back and she began trembling. It was a strange sight— she was clearly having a seizure, but there was also the appearance of ecstasy or revelation, as though some part of her had unhooked from its mooring and drifted free, and her body was floundering for purchase. The doctor held her shoulders as she shook, and he instructed the nurse to bring some drug to calm her, which was injected into her arm until the trembling stopped. She opened her eyes, drowsy.

'It looks like you just had another seizure, Lecretia,' said the doctor.

'Did I?' said Lecretia.

'Yes. I think we'll do a scan to check there are no problems in your brain, and then we'll need to prescribe you some anti-seizure medication, so that this doesn't happen again.'

Lecretia stayed in the hospital for two days after her fall. Her skull had developed a bump where she had hit it. I could feel the ridge where the skull plate had been cut, one side slightly raised, one slightly depressed, like a mountain range. The fall had knocked her around quite a bit, but she was desperate to get home. She hated being in hospital. They only let her out on the condition that Shirley would look after her, as she couldn't walk unaided or even talk properly. Lecretia didn't tell the doctors she was feeling nauseous as she was worried they would keep her in the hospital.

When she was discharged the doctors said that oncology would call, as they needed to confirm all the prescriptions she was taking were compatible. With the anti-seizure medication she was now taking a huge number of pills every day, including drugs to counteract the effects of other drugs—steroids, an anti-nausea medication and laxatives to deal with the constipating effects of the steroids. The oncology clinic never called, so Shirley followed up, as Lecretia was deteriorating. They told her to come in. We found out that when she fell she had landed on the very part of her skull that had been operated on, and the scans revealed she'd had a brain bleed. Her dosages were adjusted, and the steroids increased to reduce the swelling.

Lecretia spent a few days adjusting to the new regimen. The higher dosage of steroids was difficult for her to cope with, and the new anti-seizure medication didn't immediately agree with her—but although she was barely able to walk and felt like throwing up, she insisted that she wanted to get back to work. I think Lecretia, so defined by her career as a lawyer, saw work as something normal that she could latch on to. If she was well enough to work, she was in control of the situation. She was doing something for others. She dreaded the idea of helplessness. It just wasn't who she was.

From August 2011, things steadily improved. Lecretia's energy slowly returned, and her hair started to grow again. She wasn't having trouble getting around, she could cook and swim and dance, and she seemed like she was almost back to normal, except for that persistent blindness on her left side. But I was still worried. One night, after a couple of beers, I sat down at the computer and started writing.

> I don't know what's going to happen to Lecretia. I am so afraid. She is so beautiful and kind and this, of course, was not how we imagined things would be. I know there are statistics, and chance, and some people win the lottery and others get this. We all get something. No one has a perfect run. Or maybe a few do. But it's clear now that we are not those people. We will experience life as a fractured promise. We're the one per cent. And there is always one per cent of something, and it is not always good. History will

RIGHT: Lecretia (age eight months) with her mother, Shirley Seales, 1973

BELOW: Lecretia, bar admission with her friend Helen Spellacey (nee Salisbury), 1997

Lecretia and her parents, Larry and Shirley, brother Jeremy and sister Kat, 2002

Lecretia and
Sir Geoffrey Palmer
in Nelson,
November 2003

FROM TOP: At our wedding, April 2006, photo by Nicola Topping, Real Image; dressed up for Tim Clarke's fortieth, 2010; before surgery, March 2011

Lecretia in Aitutaki, Cook Islands, 2011

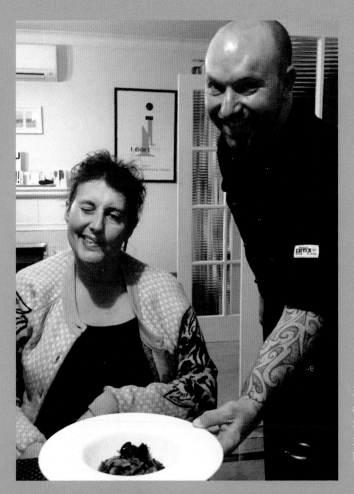

Lecretia's meal at home with chef Sam Pope, 21 May 2015, four days before her hearing

forget us, there will be no children to research our lives, to tell our stories in their classrooms. We're not destined to be ancestors of anything. I find that the hardest to deal with. I cannot bear the thought that my wife will be forgotten, that she will have no children to carry her spirit, to bear a little piece of who she is, so that a part of her continues to live on. If she dies, and let's be frank, that is on the cards, she will be lost forever, a memory for me, and for her family and friends, but then, after we all die, nothing: just a name. I suppose that will happen to most of us—it does happen to most of us. We haven't figured this out yet, have we? Some of us invent stories, or accept stories, but in our heart of hearts we know that there is an end, and it is abrupt and final, and that the divide between this and that is cold and infinite. Even people who believe in an afterlife cry at funerals.

I am worried about me, but mostly I am worried about her. I am awestruck by her bravery and how she is facing this. And even when she cries, terrified and bearing the full weight of her circumstance, it is brief, over in less than an hour, and she is sunny and cheerful again. But I know that she sits in her office caught up in her thoughts, and I know that she lies awake in bed at night while I am sleeping, and I know that though she would never want pity she must struggle with this. There's that great existential question, isn't there: if you were going to die tomorrow, what would you do? And the thing is, you probably wouldn't do anything any different, or anything more than you normally do, because the spectre of death keeps you from seizing the day you are expected to seize: you would spend your last day mourning the ones you would never have. I wonder if people reaching a certain age, suddenly aware of their decrepitude and deterioration, are filled with the same thoughts.

We went on with our everyday lives, but even in the most ordinary activities there were subtle differences. Lecretia had always loved to cook, and was an expert in the kitchen, but issues with her short-term memory started to get in the way. One night she started making dinner, but she'd forgotten to take the steaks out of the freezer, so we had to defrost them in the microwave.

'It's okay, Lecretia.'

'It's not okay. How could I be so stupid?'

'You just forgot, that's all.'

'I forget too many things now.'

I helped her finish dinner by making the kumara mash and pepper sauce. It was delicious. We sat at the table and ate together, in front of her room divider, on which she had arranged photographs from her past and our shared past. I looked at those photographs and she was still the same person. She had the same dreams, the same features—she was simply diminished. She did seem smaller. I found myself feeling so protective towards her.

After dinner I took a look at her head. Her scalp was still dry and cracked. Her hair was growing, but only on one side of her head, and at the back. The photographs of her with long hair now looked strange. I rubbed in the aloe vera, but I'm not sure it helped. Her hair seemed to absorb it, and the skin was so dry now that it appeared to have completely lifted away from the scalp, forming a bronze incrustation. It came away as large brown scabs, the size of coins, and it felt thick and waxy.

Soon after this she had lunch with her friend Carolyn. Carolyn was twenty weeks pregnant. Lecretia had given her advice about using the clinic in San Diego. They made it, we didn't. I asked Lecretia whether she was jealous. 'Yes,' she said, without hesitation.

Despite everything, Lecretia still wanted a child. I was not so certain any more. My logic was that a child would make life harder than it already was. I would end up with two dependants, and if the worst should happen, I would be a solo parent. I didn't want that. My logic, selfishly, was that if I were thrown back into a situation of having to find another partner, a child would limit my chances and my choices. And there was the child to think of too. I had been a child of divorce and loss; I came from a broken family. Could I inflict that on someone else, knowingly?

But I really didn't know anything for sure. If Lecretia wanted to be a mother, and I wanted to be a father, then maybe we should continue trying. If life made things difficult, we would deal with it. The child would be surrounded by a loving family. Children are resilient and cope with change better than adults do.

Our San Diego plans had been to use an anonymous donor, but now I thought, well, if Lecretia dies, maybe it would be better if the donor wasn't anonymous, so the child could still find out where it came from, so it could still have a sense of belonging and of its place in the world.

I discussed this with Lecretia one night. 'If the worst should happen,' I said, 'at least the child would still have a mother.'

Lecretia burst into tears. It was the worst thing I could have said, and I felt so bad. She already knew that I thought using a donor egg was somehow a lesser route, not true motherhood, but it was a reminder of my feelings, and it hurt her, and I hated to hurt her.

After Christmas 2011, things settled into a normal rhythm. Lecretia kept working at the Law Commission, and I kept working at Xero. She caught the bus at 3 pm with the school kids. I was promoted to a management role, leading the teams that built our mobile products and handled integration with banks. Xero was going gangbusters and was on the cusp of becoming a global force. The share price was steadily climbing. I fantasised about it getting so high I could sell down my holding and never have to work again. I wanted to spend time with Lecretia—I didn't want either of us to have to work.

But Lecretia felt differently. Her role at the Law Commission gave her purpose. She loved going into the office each day and she retained the respect of her colleagues. She was consumed by the work she was doing on the review of the Judicature Act 1908. When I raised the idea of her stopping work, her response was brief.

'What would I do all day?'

So we got on with the business of living. We enrolled in Spanish classes. Our theory was that learning a language might help Lecretia's brain heal. She excelled in the classes, though she hated reading off the whiteboard, or having to write on it, because she inevitably missed things. But she wasn't discouraged, and we practised at home at nights, talking in Spanish to one another.

Lecretia decided that she wanted to do dancing lessons, too, so we enrolled in tango classes. Her left leg wasn't behaving but she pushed through it, swinging her hip slightly to throw her leg forward. She loved dancing tango with me, and was able to pick up the steps, but she wasn't so much of a fan of dancing with others. When we rotated partners in our small group, she always came back into my arms with relief.

After a year of Spanish and a few months of tango, Lecretia proposed that we take a trip to Argentina together. The idea of travelling alone with Lecretia in a foreign country worried me somewhat, as she could be unsteady on her feet and got lost easily. A month earlier she'd fallen asleep on the bus home.

'Last stop,' said the driver, waking her.

'Where am I?' she asked. It was dark outside.

'You're at the last stop. You need to get off.'

'I don't know where I am.'

'Not my problem,' said the driver. 'I need to take the bus back to the depot and you can't be on it.'

Lecretia got off the bus, looking for her bearings. She pulled out her phone and it was flat. She cried tears of frustration and started walking in the direction the bus had come from. After ten minutes, she found herself in a place she recognised and was able to negotiate her way home.

Even the familiar was becoming unfamiliar. Lecretia loved doing the grocery shopping, but recently she'd started buying things we already had, or she'd get stuck in a single aisle, staring at the shelves in confusion because someone had moved the sauces section two rows over. When her favourite supermarket changed its layout it was a nightmare for her—she couldn't find anything. Our weekly trips to the supermarket became hugely frustrating for me, because it took so long, and for her, because of her disorientation. In the end, I told her it would be better if I went alone armed with lists of what she wanted. She wrote these out dutifully, but was miffed, and I would work my way through the kitchen crossing out half the items that we'd already stocked up on.

The thought of losing her in Argentina and her being unable to find her way back to the hotel on her own was frightening, so I asked Larry and Shirley to join us. They agreed and we booked our flights.

I think Lecretia was worried about her condition deteriorating, though, because she requested a scan shortly before we left. We flew out before the results arrived. We'd have to wait until our return to see whether anything had changed.

Chapter 13

BUENOS AIRES WAS a faded beauty of a city. The sons and daughters of Spanish and Italian migrants modelled their buildings on the decorous facades of their favourite Mediterranean promenades. In the prosperous suburbs of Recoleta and Palermo, gargoyles loomed from apartment buildings, and in Monserrat, a spectacular building, the Palacio Barolo, inspired by Dante's *Divine Comedy*, dominated the skyline. Huge boulevards swept through the city, the widest being Avenida 9 de Julio, as if the men who made it had come from small European cities and now found themselves blessed with the broadest canvas they could imagine.

For our seventh wedding anniversary, we found a

restaurant we liked a few blocks away from our hotel. Larry and Shirley accompanied us for dinner. We drank wine from Mendoza and ate complex and clever dishes and practised our Spanish with the waiter.

But this sprawling city was hard work for Lecretia. She walked slowly but without complaint, not letting on how tough it was for her. We visited El Ateneo Grand Splendid, a former opera house and one of the most beautiful bookshops in the world. Lecretia had barely had time to take in the sight before her legs fell from under her and she collapsed to the floor in exhaustion and wouldn't be moved.

When she had her breath back, I helped her up and held her by the arm as we left the store, and the four of us returned to the hotel via taxi.

We travelled to Bariloche, a beautiful town near the Andes, where dozens of picture-perfect lakes reflected the surrounding mountains. A short drive from the town, there was a chairlift taking you up to the summit of Cerro Campanario, an elevated peak with a full panorama of the area. We approached the chairlift.

'I'm not going on that,' said Lecretia.

'It's a long way to walk,' I said.

'I can do it,' she insisted.

We climbed over two hundred metres to the summit,

up a narrow trail of switchbacks. Lecretia pushed herself hard, ignoring the tingling in her limbs. She climbed all the way to the top. The summit offered views of the vast Andes topped with snow, and the surrounding lakes, sparkling in the sun.

In Mendoza we stayed in a beautiful bed and breakfast outside the city, where we drank red wine and ate empanadas at sunset. Lecretia's stamina was proving variable. She wandered the city of Salta without complaint. When we visited the salt flats north of Jujuy near the Bolivian border, she had trouble breathing due to the elevation. But she pushed through.

Our last stop before returning to Buenos Aires was the trip's highlight—a visit to the Iguazú Falls on the border with Brazil and Paraguay. We stayed at a hotel in the national park where the falls were visible in the distance and had two magical days exploring their majesty.

Back in New Zealand, I sat with Lecretia and showed her the photos I'd taken. The pictures of her face worried her. The left corner of her mouth had begun to droop slightly, resulting in what she called a crooked smile. It was an effect you sometimes saw in people with Bell's palsy. I was surprised I hadn't noticed it.

Walking was becoming more difficult. She was losing sensation in her left foot and ankle, which refused to bend, and needed a walking stick. She was back at work, but it was getting harder for her. Changes in technology—a new payroll system or an operating system update—would cause her stress. There was also the issue of her eyesight—she would often miss the first column of words on a page, or the first couple of words after a line break, rendering whatever she was reading nonsensical.

A few weeks after we returned, we received the results of the scans taken before Argentina. They suggested that Lecretia's tumour was beginning to grow again.

It was time to move on to the next treatment. Temozolomide was available but would be very expensive. But it turned out Merck, the pharmaceutical company, had a stockpile sitting in a warehouse unused. The temozolomide was supplied to Lecretia compassionately, at no cost, and to several other cancer patients besides. I was filled with a huge amount of gratitude for Merck.

Lecretia began taking temozolomide in May, less than a month after we had returned from Argentina, but it didn't arrest her decline immediately. We added clomipramine, a drug that had been shown to reduce the size of tumours in mice, and Salvestrol, a plant extract that some believed had anti-cancer properties. Neither drug had significant side effects so Lecretia had nothing to lose by taking them.

She was still insisting on getting herself to and from work alone, but after a couple of close calls, I organised to leave work at 3 pm, drive to her office and pick her up. I'd log into work from home, finishing up at around 6.30 or 7 pm, when I'd cook dinner if Lecretia hadn't managed to do so. It was a busy time.

After a couple of months, however, the combination of drugs that Lecretia was taking began to kick in, and her movement improved. She stopped using the walking stick. She was brighter. She started to go to work on her own again. In October 2013 we travelled to Queenstown together, and stayed at the fanciest hotel we could find, right on the lakefront, and we went to beautiful restaurants. Lecretia watched as I experienced the luge, and when I did a bungy jump from the Kawarau River Bridge.

By November Lecretia was well enough to resume catching the bus home. I was nervous about it, but she insisted. She hated being dependent on others, being dependent on me. For her, the troughs of her illness were temporary inconveniences to be recovered from as quickly as possible so that she could resume her normal life.

Her independence helped me, too. My career was taking off at Xero. I had restructured the mobile team and expanded the banking team, and was now responsible for the work of over twenty people. I was being called on to speak at company conferences, and to travel overseas to meet with Australian and American banking partners. When I had to travel, friends and family would come and stay with Lecretia. She would insist that she could look after herself, but I knew that wasn't true. I think she knew it too, because after a short protest she would relent, and she was not someone who would give in easily.

I'm ashamed to say that these excursions were sometimes welcome breaks. It was tough looking after Lecretia at home on my own, and when I went overseas I had some time to recharge and find my way back to appreciating my wife and loving her in a renewed way, so that when I came home I could be with her completely. It's true that absence makes the heart grow fonder. I suppose in that respect it's similar to grief.

Lecretia wanted to come with me on some of these excursions, as my work took me to places like Sydney or Melbourne or Los Angeles or San Francisco, but I worried about her being alone while I worked. In unfamiliar surroundings she would become hopelessly lost, and incapable of getting the help she needed.

Nevertheless, I organised with Lecretia's friend Hilary to meet us in San Francisco while I was on a work trip there. Hilary was based in Bermuda, and the agreement was that we would meet her in San Francisco for a weekend, after which Lecretia would go to Bermuda with Hilary and I would stay in the US for work.

In San Francisco I took Lecretia to Atelier Crenn, a restaurant holding two Michelin stars, where a single meal cost me more than a week's salary, but whose chef was an utter artist. Her dishes were the most imaginative I have ever encountered. The menu was a seventeen-line poem. As a diner, Lecretia preferred taste and texture over spectacle, but this was one of the best meals of our lives.

In Bermuda I found my wife in the picture of health. She had spent most days sunning herself at the beach and enjoying the fresh Bermuda seafood with Hilary and her children.

Back in New Zealand in August 2013, it was clear that Lecretia's ability to walk was deteriorating again. The tumour was starting to resist the effects of the chemotherapy. The oncologist insisted that temozolomide was no longer providing any sort of tangible benefit, and that we should not continue with it.

Despite this, Lecretia decided that after she stopped taking temozolomide, we deserved another holiday, this time in Morocco. I was worried about terrorism—some of the ISIL soldiers in Iraq and Syria had come from

Morocco, and had threatened to bring its reactionary brand of fundamentalism home—but Lecretia was fearless. She could no longer read outside work—it took too much effort—but she devoured audiobooks. She would listen to them in bed while she went to sleep. Her two favourite audiobooks were a history of the papacy—a litany of scandal and abuse—and *A Concise History of the Middle East*, the 'concise' part of the title being ironic, as the print version was more than five hundred pages long.

In listening to this, she built up a more nuanced understanding of Islam and the Middle East and was not worried about visiting Morocco in the slightest.

We scheduled our flights in early October. Larry and Shirley agreed to join us again. Given our experience in Argentina, we arranged a private tour this time, so we'd have our own driver and all the accommodation would be booked.

We flew to Casablanca via Abu Dhabi, and landed in the morning. We were driven first to Rabat, the capital of Morocco, about two hours away. Our driver, Namir, was a pleasant man with a receding hairline who wore a black shirt and beige trousers. He immediately saw that Lecretia needed assistance with a few things, such as getting into our SUV. We talked about Morocco and our cultural differences, and he was kind and open with us.

After a night in Rabat we travelled to Chefchaouen, a beautiful mountain town where all the houses were painted a cool sky blue in honour of the town's Jewish heritage, as Jews were allowed to settle there after they and the Muslims were expelled from Spain.

We stayed in a place up on the hillside. Unfortunately it had three flights of stairs, and Lecretia struggled with them. Larry and I took her by the arm as she slowly climbed up or down. Every excursion to the restaurant upstairs or to explore the city below meant negotiating these steps. But when we sat on the rooftop under the clear sky, waiting for dinner, I saw her face light up as the sun shone on the arid hills around us, bathing the deep blue terraced dwellings of the town in light, as the muezzins called out their evening prayers from the minarets and the whole place seemed to bow in worship.

In Fes we visited the city's giant medina, or old Arab quarter. It was criss-crossed with narrow alleys and lanes and tunnels, designed to confuse invaders and certainly confusing for a young woman with brain cancer, but it was still a delight for her. We went to a cooking school there and learned to make a tagine: chicken with olives and preserved lemon. I teased Lecretia that the tagine was the poor cousin of the casserole, but she wouldn't have that. She diligently tasted every tagine at each restaurant as if it were being tried for the first time, mentally taking notes so she might recreate the best possible version of the dish at home.

We then headed to Erfoud, and took a four-wheel drive out to the Sahara in the late afternoon. We rode camels into the dunes, and looked out over the burnished expanse of sand. I had always wanted to see the Sahara, without really knowing why. What I felt was impermanence, as the wind lifted sand off the crests to rest in the shallows, forming new crests and gullies. We felt very small, but utterly present, alive and together in an alien place. I put my arm around Lecretia and we sat quietly taking it all in. Time is the only thing we truly possess, and even that runs through our fingers like a handful of dust. How grateful I was to be there in that moment, to have found this person I loved, and who loved me.

We camped that night in the desert. The stars were abundantly clear and the silence absolute. That night, I held Lecretia close, and I slept the best I had ever slept in my life.

In Marrakesh we stayed at an incredible riad—a traditional Moroccan house—and I fell in love with Arabic architecture. When you live in a riad, your home is truly a sanctuary. They have few exterior windows; instead there is a central courtyard, open to the sky, and all the rooms face into that yard. It really feels like an escape from the outside world.

At this point, Lecretia's ability to climb stairs was becoming much more limited. But when we got to the seaside town of Essaouira she wandered around the city, venturing with me down to the ancient docks, where seagulls sprinkled the stones with guano as they circled hungrily.

That night we dined at a restaurant close to the hotel. After every meal, Lecretia would take a cocktail of pills: Salvestrol, levothyroxine for her thyroid, turmeric, clomipramine, levetiracetam. She would swallow these without complaint, though she would often sit back with her eyes closed and savour what she'd just eaten first, before taking the bitter tablets.

Our tour finished with lunch at Rick's Café in Casablanca, where the classic film starring Bogart and Bergman was set. Years earlier, when Lecretia was well, we had watched the film together at an outdoor cinema in a vineyard in Hawkes Bay. I remember she wore a thick blue fleece hoodie, because even though it was summer, it was a cold evening. We would never have dreamt that we would one day be here in Casablanca, eating lunch where Rick and Ilsa had their unrequited reunion before saying goodbye. But nor would we have dreamt of the struggles on staircases, the pills, the tiredness, the confusion and the frustration.

Inside the Hassan II Mosque in Casablanca, we saw the polished wooden floor and the carpets and the glass windows and the retracting ceiling and every surface covered in calligraphy—the words of the prophet Mohammed, and through him, his god. I felt the same feelings as at the Vatican all those years ago, the sense of a warp in the tapestry so great that the knot obscured the truth of its binding.

Rumi, the Persian poet and Sufi mystic, tells a story about several men in a dark room each touching an elephant and being asked to describe what it is: the man touching the trunk says a waterspout, the man touching the ear says a fan, the man touching the leg says a pillar, the man touching its back says a throne. Each is sure of his convictions.

Judaism, Christianity, Islam—each the palm of a hand on a different part of God. Which man do you trust when we are all in the dark? How is it that where I am born or who I believe might condemn me? When I look at these holy sites, I see humanity's desperate yearning for meaning, and how we cleave to the seduction of metaphor in the stories we tell ourselves. How beautiful these stories are, and how amazing that some people find them so seductive they will build lives and empires around them.

The flight home was long and arduous. Shirley and I walked Lecretia up and down the plane to stretch her legs, and she staggered up the aisles slowly, her left leg clearly less responsive than it had been. Her left arm too was now weak, and she had trouble gripping the edge of the seats as she passed them.

A few days after we returned, Lecretia went back to work. She was giving advice on a review of New Zealand's contempt of court legislation. She confessed to me now how difficult she found it: the words on her computer screen and on the pages in front of her were swimming disturbingly.

We went to her oncologist in November, and Lecretia scheduled her first round of her new chemotherapy, a mix of procarbazine and lomustine, which were older and harsher drugs than temozolomide. She wrote to her friends:

Hello gorgeous friends,

I just wanted to reiterate that I am embarking on my new chemo regimen on Monday in a positive frame of mind. The fight is not over!

I would, however, like each of you to watch the clip of Terry Pratchett in the link below to get a sense of what I may want further down the track.

I may become active in this area ...

I love you all so much and could never have got this far without you. You're my besties!

L xx

The link she included was to a lecture given in 2010 by Sir Terry Pratchett, the novelist, assisted by the actor Tony Robinson, called *Shaking Hands with Death*. In it, Sir Terry describes his struggles with progressive Alzheimer's, and his experience of being aware of slowly losing his mind. He explores the inevitability of his death and how it is a horror to him, and how, given his values and the way he'd lived, there was a conflict between the way he wished to die and the way he likely would. Through Tony, he illustrates sitting in his garden, listening to music, and taking some modern hemlock to bring himself to a peaceful end.

Chapter 14

LECRETIA HAD NOT spoken of her death much with me. She was focused on getting better, and managing her illness, but since Morocco it had come up a little more often. That may have been because the new regimen of procarbazine and lomustine would squash any hope that we could have children. Now she started talking about ifs.

If she were to die, she wanted me to move on, find someone else, have a family, perhaps move overseas and see more of the world. If she were to die, maybe she would prefer to be cremated rather than buried. If she were to die, she wanted to be interred near her grandparents.

But all the speculation seemed ridiculous: there was too much she wanted to do. Her contempt of court project wasn't finished. She hadn't yet been to India, and had started making inquiries about a guided tour there. She was determined to speak at her mother's sixtieth birthday in 2016, and to see her beloved sister Kat have a baby.

Though she was still well, I had resumed taking Lecretia home from work in the afternoons because she couldn't lift her legs high enough to get on the bus any more. It was heartbreaking to see her stagger across the road to meet me. When she got into the passenger seat, I had to lift her legs into the car. But this was nothing more than an inconvenience for her. It was a long way from a terminal decline.

And yet the actual manner of Lecretia's death, whenever it happened, was of concern to her. In late 2014, a member of parliament, Iain Lees-Galloway, was canvassing support for an End of Life Choice bill. Lecretia researched the bill and was supportive of it—it allowed for something called an advance directive, which would allow a person to specify their end-of-life wishes before they reached a point where they were no longer competent to do so. Those wishes could include euthanasia.

Assisted dying was not legal in New Zealand, and only legal in a few countries. Australia was the first country in the world to have assisted-dying laws, passing them in the Northern Territory in 1995, but the territorial law was overruled at the federal level shortly afterwards. In the US state of Oregon, assisted-dying laws came into effect in 1997, making it legal for a doctor to prescribe life-ending medication to a terminally ill patient with less than six months to live. Oregon has had its laws in place the longest of any jurisdiction in the world.

Belgium and the Netherlands passed laws allowing assisted dying in 2002, permitting doctors to administer life-ending medication with a patient's consent. Luxembourg followed in 2008. Several other US states legalised assisted dying from that same year onwards, either through explicit legislation or court rulings.

Switzerland, interestingly, has never had explicit laws permitting assisted dying, but since 1942 it has only been a crime to help someone commit suicide if your motive is selfish. Private groups have formed there to help people suffering terminal illness or unendurable pain to plan an assisted death: they can arrange access to cooperative doctors and life-ending medications that patients self-administer. Dignitas, perhaps the most famous association of its type, has been in operation in Switzerland since 1998.

New Zealand is a fairly forward-thinking nation. It was the first country in the world to give women the vote and it has legalised gay marriage and abortion. Freedom of religion is something we have always taken for granted, but it was formally enshrined in our bill of rights in 1990. Holding back on assisted dying seemed to go against New Zealand's values of fairness, pragmatism and tolerance.

Lecretia wrote an opinion piece to support her views.

When I was first diagnosed with brain cancer, I was told I would only have weeks to live unless I had urgent surgery. That was three and a half years ago, when I was thirty-seven years old.

Over the ensuing years, I have had brain surgery to prune the tumour, as well as radiation therapy and chemotherapy in a bid to control the growth of the tumour. I have recently embarked on a different chemo-therapy regimen, and remain very hopeful that this will stave things off for another few years. Ultimately, though, there is only one way my story can end.

Life is not the same as it was pre-cancer. I am unable to see anything left of centre. The left side of my body does not move very well. I have difficulty walking, typing with my left hand and eating with a knife and fork. I require assistance from my husband to get dressed each morning. I am not allowed to drive. I have lost spatial awareness and get lost easily in new places. I constantly bump into things. My balance has been affected and I have falls like an old woman. My head is scarred and bald in patches from radiation burns. From time to time I have searing headaches. My dreams for the future have been dashed.

And yet I still have so much to be thankful for. My cognitive ability has not been affected, so I am able to continue working as a senior legal and policy adviser at the Law Commission, albeit with shorter hours, as I tire easily. I am presently the lead adviser on the commission's review of contempt of court.

Being near death prompted an outpouring of love and support from friends and family that most people never have the opportunity to experience in their lifetime. I continue to live my life to the fullest, including travelling to exotic and exciting places, and I have wonderful friends and family to share my precious time with.

I am not afraid of dying but I am petrified by what may happen to me in the lead-up to my death. My greatest fear is losing my mental faculties and leaving my husband with a mad wife to deal with, like Mr Rochester in *Jane Eyre*. As far as I'm concerned, if I get to a point where I can no longer recognise or communicate with my husband, then for all intents and purposes I will already be dead. Why string out the process of actually dying? Nor do I wish to be a prisoner in my own body, unable to move and lying in my own excrement. That's not a dignified way to die!

Why can't we make informed choices regarding the timing and manner of our death, so death is as pleasant a process as possible?

I believe it is a fundamental human right to choose to die when life will become intolerable because of the effects of a terminal illness or debilitating condition. I'm not sure I could actually exercise that right if I had it, but I should at least have the choice.

I would get that choice if MP Iain Lees-Galloway's End of Life Choice bill were selected in the members bill ballot and passed by parliament. It would provide individuals with a choice to end their lives and to receive medical assistance to die under certain circumstances. To qualify, the person making the request for assistance to die ('the applicant') must be a New Zealand citizen or resident aged eighteen years or over who is mentally competent, as attested by two medical practitioners.

The applicant must also suffer from either a terminal disease or other medical condition that is likely to end his or her life within twelve months, or an irreversible physical or mental medical condition that, in the applicant's view, renders his or her life unbearable.

A request for medical assistance to die must be made in writing, signed by the applicant and confirmed in writing by the applicant after a cooling-off period of at least seven days.

Research by Horizon Research on New Zealanders' views on end-of-life choices conducted in July 2012 showed that 62.9 per cent of adult New Zealanders support entitling all mentally competent adults to receive medical assistance in ending their life if they are suffering from a terminal illness or an irreversible physical or mental condition that in their view renders their life unbearable. I would hazard a guess that that figure would now be higher, following the film segment made and distributed via social media by brain cancer patient Brittany Maynard.

Being in pain and unable to move is a misery, not a life. As my aunt, who is a nurse, has said to me, 'lingering is not living'.

When a person is terminally ill, there may only be a brief period when that person is able to make rational and sensible decisions and is physically able to sign a form or self-administer a lethal drug. That is where assisted dying in accordance with previously recorded wishes should be possible. The bill provides for this too by establishing a regime for the registration and implementation of an end-of-life directive made by a person who is terminally ill while that person is mentally competent, but to be actioned after the person becomes mentally incompetent or other specified circumstances exist. Without such a regime, a person who is terminally ill has only the option of committing suicide while they are physically able to, which may be long before an end-of-life directive would have come into effect. Suicide is a lonely and often violent death. It would be far more humane to enable a peaceful process for dying surrounded by loved ones.

Although I am not suggesting for one moment that the most appropriate lens for examining this type of situation is an economic one, an economic analysis supports the humanist view. From an economic perspective, it would be madness to pay to keep someone alive and in care when the person does not even want this. It would be far better to allocate that funding to another part of our overstretched health care system.

Several other countries allow mentally competent, terminally ill residents to voluntarily request and receive aid to hasten their death. It is time for New Zealand to catch up and recognise the right to have an end-of-life choice.

Lecretia sent the article to her friend Cate Brett, asking her whether she thought a newspaper might be willing to publish it. Cate suggested sharing it with her friend, the renowned journalist Rebecca Macfie. Rebecca called Lecretia and asked if she could write a story about her for the *Listener*. Lecretia agreed.

I advised Lecretia against doing the piece. I couldn't understand why she wanted to give up her privacy, and I was rather selfishly worried for myself. My career was beginning to take off at Xero, and I was concerned about what it might mean for me if I was pulled into the story. I was also worried about how I might be perceived—that if my voice were too strongly supportive, people might wonder whether I was pushing Lecretia towards this point of view, or worse, coercing her into seeking assisted death. But I began to see that Lecretia's inner strength and discipline—previously focused on maintaining privacy, dignity and strength in the face of pain and diminishment—were now being devoted to injustice. She wanted to galvanise law reform.

The story, 'Dying Wishes', was published in January 2015, just a few weeks after Iain Lees-Galloway was instructed by his party leader, Andrew Little, to withdraw his private member's bill from consideration. The End of Life Choice bill was history, but Lecretia's quest to change the law had begun.

Chapter 15

AS LECRETIA AND I faced her illness, and the prospect that her treatment options were running out, I found that I began throwing myself into work. I leaned more heavily on Lecretia's friends and family to support her at home. This was partially because work had become much more demanding, involving more international travel, but at the same time I was certain Lecretia wouldn't be able to work much longer and that our income would be pulled back. I didn't know what costs were likely to arise in having to care for her. I felt like I had to do whatever it took to keep my role at Xero. The common wisdom is that health problems put work into perspective and make it less important, but that's not true: in the absence of complete financial freedom, something most young people will never have, they increase your reliance on work to ensure your continued comfort. I wanted to make sure Lecretia had everything she needed, and that was only going to be possible with a good income. Of course I wanted to stay home with her, but we lived in the real world.

When an opportunity came up to go to Vancouver in Canada in early 2015 for a leadership training program, I asked Lecretia what she thought.

'You should do it,' she said.

She didn't want me to go, but we always shared a basic principle in our marriage: never hold the other back. Nonetheless, I felt guilt. But my view was that Lecretia was going to live for another eighteen months at least, perhaps longer, and that if she got *really* ill, I might not get this opportunity again. We might both be off work for years as I cared for her at home. We couldn't predict the future. So we agreed I would go to Vancouver.

The day Lecretia's story was published in the *Listener*, I was heading to Auckland to connect to a flight to San Francisco. I picked up five copies of the magazine at the airport. I remember the strange sensation of seeing Lecretia's face staring out from the magazine rack, the first flicker of her fame. She looked beautiful. The only hint of her illness was a slight weakness in one side of her smile.

Lecretia's central argument at that time was that the Law Commission, her employer, was the best forum in which to explore the issue of assisted dying. Under Sir Geoffrey Palmer's leadership it had taken on more social issues—like a review of the legislation regulating the sale and supply of liquor—and had proven itself adept at handling such things. Lecretia's view was that the Law Commission could evaluate the evidence dispassionately and make sound recommendations on how the law might be amended to achieve desirable social outcomes, which would form the basis of an informed parliamentary debate.

At that point, Cate Brett offered to handle media for Lecretia, fielding requests for interviews, comments and statements. We trusted her completely. After the article's publication, there were inquiries from most of New Zealand's major news sources, and many letters from New Zealanders in support of Lecretia's stand.

Lecretia's first course of action was to write to the minister of justice, Amy Adams, requesting that the government refer the issue to the Law Commission for investigation. The minister's office didn't reply to Lecretia directly, to my knowledge, but called the chief commissioner, Sir Grant Hammond, to ask what this was all about. It became pretty clear that the Ministry of Justice was not going to request an inquiry, and that the Law Commission was not going to upset the government of the day by initiating its own inquiry into such a fraught area.

Meanwhile, I began my leadership course in Vancouver, in the heart of the Canadian winter. It had brought together twenty-four people, mostly from the US and Canada, from various disciplines. The course took a holistic approach that encompassed meditation, diet and soul-searching as well as practical exercises in creative direction and leadership.

On the first day, after taking a long walk along the beach, we came upon a Fibonacci spiral of small disks, laid out in the sand. One by one, we were told to walk the spiral outwards, as slow as we liked. Each stepping stone represented a year of our lives, and we were to reflect on the person we were at each step, and to stop on the year we were currently in.

When it was my turn, I remembered the cheeky, big-eared kid I was, my years in primary school, my awkward teenage years of bad poetry and desperately wanting to escape being a misfit. The pain of my parents' divorce, my bacchanalian university years in Auckland, moving to Wellington and starting to come right. I remembered my feeling of not completely being in sync with the world until Lecretia appeared when I was twenty-six. I was imagining walking with her, recalling the experience of falling in love with her, of marrying her. I smiled with every step. And then remembering those three years of struggling with fertility, and Lecretia's longing to conceive. Her illness, and the memory of sharing our lives as it took hold of her; the years of radiotherapy and chemotherapy and doctors' visits and letters to overseas clinics and late night conversations about the future.

When my feet came to rest on the thirty-eighth stone, I stopped. In walking the spiral I'd had a sense of being on a trajectory, and Lecretia being on that trajectory with me—but somewhere beyond the stone I was on, I would probably be walking alone again. And it scared me.

I was told to walk back to the point where my life had most significantly changed. I walked back four years, to where Lecretia had gotten ill. I briefly considered walking back to when I had met her, or when we married. But those things hadn't changed me. When she met me, and when she married me, Lecretia accepted me for who I was, although she did make me want to be a better person. When she got ill, however, the trajectory of my life was inexorably disrupted. My own view of myself changed from partner to provider, from lover to carer. I took my job more seriously. I became more ambitious—not to secure my own success, but to ensure I would be able to provide for her. It was at that point that the future had suddenly became chaotic: images of kids and white picket fences and retirement and growing old together were broken into fragments shored against the ruins of our future, which was a wasteland.

And then I walked out to where I thought my life would end. I walked out along the spiral arm to eighty-three, and looked back to where thirty-eight was, and wondered how many more steps from there I would have Lecretia with me. I hoped for decades.

At around this time a hearing was drawing to an end in the Supreme Court of Canada. In 2012, in a landmark ruling in the Supreme Court of British Columbia, Justice Lynn Smith had declared that the prohibition on assisted dying was unconstitutional, and that the government was obliged to amend the law to allow it. After the most exhaustive review of the evidence ever conducted, examining what had happened in Oregon, Washington, Vermont and Montana, along with the Netherlands and Belgium, Justice Smith decided that there was nothing to suggest that the various nightmare scenarios presented by anti-assisted-dying advocates had come to pass. On the contrary, she found that most objections were really only arguments for stronger safeguards. She declared the criminal provisions that prevented assisted dying in Canada were unconstitutional, finding them an infringement of every Canadian's right to life, liberty and security of the person.

In 2014, the case went to the Supreme Court of Canada, the highest court in the land, and in February 2015 its nine judges unanimously upheld the judgment of Justice Lynn Smith. The Canadian government was then forced to implement assisted-dying laws in accordance with Justice Smith's original ruling, which would take effect in June 2016.

When I returned home it was a happy reunion, but I noted the difference in Lecretia's condition. She was a little unsteadier now, and had taken to using her walking stick more and more. She was still as determined as ever, though, and the case in Canada had caught her interest.

In New Zealand, identifying an infringement of rights was not enough to change the law like it could in Canada, but what a court case could achieve is something called a declaration of inconsistency. If a judge ruled that the bill of rights and a particular law were not consistent, there would be impetus for parliament to clarify the laws to deal with it. Lecretia mused that a declaration here might lead to a debate in the house and a select committee review, meaning that the public could finally have their say. If a declaration of inconsistency could be achieved in the courts, parliament would almost certainly be spurred into some sort of action. The only problem was that since the enactment of the Bill of Rights Act in 1990, no New Zealand court had ever made a declaration of inconsistency.

Lecretia's interest in the New Zealand bill of rights was longstanding. In 2006, she co-wrote an article for *NZ Lawyer* magazine: 'An Underutilised Public Law Tool? The First 15 Years of the New Zealand Bill of Rights Act 1990'. In it she drew attention to the fact that the use of the bill of rights in the civil arena had so far been limited.

Lecretia contacted Andrew Butler, a lawyer specialising in public and constitutional law who practised at Russell McVeagh and was a leading expert on New Zealand's bill of rights, to sound him out about what had happened in Canada:

Hi Andrew,

You are probably too busy to entertain this but I thought I would sow the seed anyway. You may be aware that the Canadian Supreme Court has very recently held by a unanimous 9:0 decision that laws banning assisted dying in that country are unconstitutional. It would be interesting to see what our own courts might have to say on the matter.

If anyone was interested in taking a potentially groundbreaking case on, I would be an ideal plaintiff because the issue is of direct relevance to me. I don't have deep pockets however!

Andrew replied to Lecretia, and they had a long discussion about it, but made no firm commitments. She emailed him again:

> Thanks for talking to me today. I've spoken to my GP, who would be willing to assist me if granted immunity from prosecution for aiding suicide.
>
> I should say that I am nowhere near the point where I would want assistance to die, but it would be a comfort to know it was available should things become too awful.

Lecretia was interviewed in early March on Radio New Zealand. I helped her dress and took her to the studio. Once she was collected at reception, I went out to the car to find a better park. It took me fifteen minutes to find one, and I remember listening to the radio as I did so, and hearing my wife's voice as she began talking about her beliefs and why she was campaigning for change. Her conviction and her self-belief were unmistakable. What she was saying was coming straight from the heart. She really wanted to have the choice to be assisted to die, and she sensed a great injustice.

Lecretia was asked about the Canadian court decision, which had happened less than a month ago, and whether a similar decision could be reached in New Zealand. Lecretia replied that one could.

She still wasn't sure about taking the case, as her health was continuing to get worse. After three rounds of chemotherapy, with no beneficial effects, the oncologist could offer no further treatment. Though Lecretia seemed willing to accept this, her mother and I pleaded with the oncologist for other options, but after treatment Lecretia's white blood cell count was dangerously low, and it had to recover before we could look at anything else. For the time being, all treatment, except for anti-seizure medication and steroids for swelling, had ceased.

Later in March, we headed south to Christchurch to catch up with Cate for an evening. The next day we drove to Kaikoura, on the east coast of the South Island, to go whale-watching. We stayed in a lodge just north of the town, and had a beautiful spacious room in the main building. We were up some steps, but they were shallow enough for Lecretia to ascend them. We ate dinner at the lodge, and it occurred to me how normal things were when we sat down together like this. The only assistance she needed was for me to cut her food up for her, so that she could manage with a fork in her right hand. Her left hand could no longer grasp one.

'I'm going to take this case,' she said. She had talked about it with me before, but speculatively, as though weighing up the pros and cons. But clearly she'd made a decision now.

'Babe, are you sure? Do you really want to put yourself through this?'

'Someone has to do it. Besides, it's really interesting. New Zealand hasn't had a case like this before.'

'I understand why you need to speak to the media to raise the profile of the issue. But why would you want to go near a court? They're horrible places.'

'They're not,' she said. 'I *like* courts. This is important.'

'But it'll be all over the news. There's your privacy to consider. There are weirdos out there. Do you really want that sort of attention? I don't want to be opening mail with threats from fundamentalists.'

'If not me, who? The government won't go near this. If this works, they'll have to. It'll be fun.'

She had a strange idea of fun, in my opinion, and I told her so.

'Well, keep me out of it,' I said. 'I don't want people thinking I'm pushing you into it.'

'They won't think that, silly.'

'They will. You see someone on TV with an illness, doing something like this, and you start to suspect the person beside them. I don't want people thinking I'm manipulating you.'

'That's ridiculous. It's my case. You won't even be involved.'

It was clear she wouldn't be dissuaded. I was worried about the effect the case might have on my career. Would people doorstop us at our home? Would people try to hurt her? I could bear anything but the thought of Lecretia getting hurt, especially in her current condition. What if my wife fronted up to this and the media took a tough line on her? What if they assassinated her character? It happened all the time. I'd never met anyone as decent, as honest, as pure of heart as my wife. But this issue was so explosive I knew there was a chance that someone would try to malign her. My urge was to protect her, but even now, who was I to hold her back from something she clearly wanted?

Chapter 16

THE SEA WAS looking rough the next morning, which meant the whale-watching expedition was cancelled. We were flying back to Wellington that afternoon.

Lecretia was devastated. She'd been talking about seeing the whales at Kaikoura for years. She had a soft spot for big mammals. At Taronga Zoo in Sydney a few years ago she'd stood with her face pressed to the glass of the gorilla enclosure, eyes alight with adoration. It took a long time to talk her out of holidaying in Uganda after that.

I promised her we would be back one day to try again. She didn't seem convinced. Perhaps she sensed this was her last chance.

Instead we explored the seal colony at the promontory at the end of the township. We ate crayfish at a roadside stall, and then stopped at a winery for lunch. Lecretia gingerly found her way to the only free table, in the far corner of the restaurant. I sat to her left, where she couldn't see me, but which allowed her to see the waitstaff approaching and the other people in the restaurant.

After lunch, Lecretia spent longer in the bathroom than I'd expected, and time got away from us. We were going to struggle to get to Christchurch airport on time. We arrived very late, beyond the advertised check-in time, and despite Lecretia's protests I secured a wheelchair for her and ran through the airport to the departure gate pushing her in front of me. It must have looked like I was giving her a joyride. I was thoroughly stressed about the whole thing: I am not one of those people who can abide rushing for flights, and we very nearly missed it.

Once seated in the plane, Lecretia turned to me, smiling mischievously, and said: 'See? Nothing to worry about.' To this day I think she always wanted to miss that flight and get another chance to see the whales.

When we returned, Lecretia resumed discussing the case with Andrew Butler. Until then he hadn't committed to taking it on, but she was doing her best to convince him. Part of his hesitation was the fact that he was a Catholic.

It perplexed me too—why did Lecretia want a Catholic to lead her case? But she was convinced he was the best lawyer for the job.

After Kaikoura, Andrew was able to see how committed she was, and he agreed to propose it to the other partners at Russell McVeagh to get their support. Though Lecretia and I would pay part of the cost, the bulk of the case would be pro bono and funded by the law firm. The cost of a High Court case generally runs into hundreds of thousands of dollars, so it was no surprise that the partners were hesitant to take it on.

However, when Mai Chen, Lecretia's former employer at Chen Palmer, expressed interest in taking the case, the decision became an easier one for the partners at Russell McVeagh to make. Taking on a pro bono case was one thing, but losing the opportunity to take on a high-profile pro bono case to a rival law firm was quite another. After Lecretia let Andrew know about Mai's interest in the case, he got back to her quickly to say that the partners were now fully supportive and explain how he saw things going ahead. He proposed a timeline and a figure for our financial contribution, and gave Lecretia and I time to talk it over.

Lecretia sent him a short email the next morning, with the subject line 'Let's go':

Hi Andrew,

I just wanted to confirm that I'd like to go ahead with proceedings in the way we discussed yesterday.

On 13 March 2015 he accepted instructions to take the case to the High Court, and to file a statement of claim about Lecretia's right to have a doctor assist her to die.

Lecretia was still very independent, rejecting assistance except where there was a tacit agreement that I would help: getting dressed, cooking, helping her up to the car and in and out of it. When I tried to help in a new way, she was always resistant; I suppose each additional thing she wasn't able to do was a cause for concern.

But there were times when she took a tumble. Sometimes she'd try getting up by herself, or moving from one room to another. In our home was a short, narrow hallway, and with the left side of her vision not working, she would find herself bumping into the left-hand side of the corridor, or into the left-hand side of a doorframe. She was prone to falling through them.

On one particular night in March, Lecretia was in the hallway. She spotted Ferdinand at the other end and sang to him as she often did. He blinked at her in the way that cats do. She turned to her left and clipped her nose on the door, lost her balance and fell into the living room, landing with a thump on the floor. Blood started gushing from a cut on the side of her nose, making a thick red puddle on the carpet. I was cooking in the kitchen. Hearing her fall I rushed in to see her curled up in a foetal position, the blood pooling around her head. She was whimpering and crying.

I knelt at her side and tried to lift her, but whether through shock or weakness she didn't want to move.

'Oh babe, what did you do?'

'I fell.'

'I'll get you something, hang on.'

I went and got a damp cloth, then propped her up in a sitting position and held the cloth to her nose. The cut was only small, but it produced a lot of blood, and she complained of it hurting. As she never complained, I was worried. In a little while she gathered the strength to let me help pick her up, and I got her to the couch. These falls were becoming more frequent.

Every morning, she did floor exercises, trying to build up her strength. She stretched her legs and her arms and did sit-ups. And she used to get herself up by pushing her good arm against the side of the couch. But not any more. If she fell, she was helpless.

Could my wife, so diminished, so helpless, really face a court case and everything that went with it?

Once we'd decided to file a claim in the High Court, Cate started to brief journalists. I set up a Facebook page called *Lecretia's Choice* and posted a link to Rebecca Macfie's January *Listener* article. Within a couple of hours I had a few hundred likes. The social media campaign had begun.

The team at Russell McVeagh consisted of Andrew Butler, the lead counsel, Chris Curran, a smart young human rights lawyer, and Lecretia's friend and former colleague from Chen Palmer, Catherine Marks. Russell McVeagh set out two claims. The first was that the Crimes Act did not prohibit a doctor from helping Lecretia to die. Suicide in New Zealand is not illegal, but aiding and abetting of suicide is, with a maximum jail term of fourteen years. This claim leaned on the fact that there is no definition of suicide in the New Zealand Crimes Act, and that what Lecretia wanted the right to do did not constitute suicide, and therefore a doctor helping her would not be breaking the law. The other argument this claim relied on was that the doctor's intent would be to end suffering, not to take a life.

There had never been a case like it in New Zealand, and it was unusual in that it was a priori, or before the fact. Lecretia was attempting to ascertain the legality of an act bringing about the end of her life before the act had taken place. Most court cases in New Zealand that had dealt with the legal definitions of assisted suicide or murder took place after those events had happened. It was only then, with one life lost, and another potentially ruined, that the bounds of those definitions were tested.

Though no doctor in New Zealand had been charged with helping a consenting patient to die, there had been cases in New Zealand of family members assisting their terminally ill or suffering relatives to end their lives. Lesley Martin, a former nurse, famously helped her mother to die by injecting her with a lethal dose of morphine in 1999. She was investigated at the time, but no charges were laid until three years later, when she published a book, *To Die Like a Dog*, in which she bravely gave details of her role in her mother's death. She was arrested, tried and sentenced to fifteen months of home detention.

Professor Sean Davison helped his mother, Pat, to die in 2006. His mother, a doctor, had given her son instructions on the right medication to provide her to end her life, and after much soul-searching, he agreed to do so. He was sentenced to five months of home detention. After he was freed, he left for South Africa, where he founded DignitySA and began campaigning for assisted-dying law changes there.

Evans Mott helped his wife Rosie to die in 2011. She suffered from multiple sclerosis. He helped her procure the means to end her own life, and on her instructions he left the house while she did so. Mr Mott was arrested and prosecuted but discharged without conviction.

In each of these cases the judiciary showed a certain leniency, giving light sentences or no sentence at all because the defendant was motivated by compassion—but could a doctor be successfully prosecuted for assisting the death of a patient in Lecretia's specific circumstances, if they had the consent of that patient and the intent was to curtail the suffering of that patient? Lecretia intended to test this in the courts.

Lecretia's second claim was that the Crimes Act— if it did imply that a doctor helping her to die could be successfully prosecuted—infringed the rights granted to her under New Zealand's bill of rights, specifically the right to life. The argument was that Lecretia, denied the right to an assisted death, would have to consider taking her own life early, without assistance, and while she still could. She also had the right not to be subjected to cruel, degrading or disproportionately severe treatment, which the lack of assisted-dying laws essentially forced her to undergo. If the High Court found that the Crimes Act was inconsistent with New Zealand's bill of rights, it would, Lecretia hoped, prompt parliament to legislate to remove the inconsistency—which was what had happened in Canada.

The first claim would be tough to win, but it was Lecretia's only real hope. If the judge ruled that a doctor wouldn't be prosecuted, then Lecretia's GP could safely help her to die—if she requested it. Winning the second claim wouldn't help Lecretia, as any changes to the law would come too late for her, but it would advance the debate in New Zealand by years, if not decades.

Cate and I drafted a press release outlining the claims. Lecretia wrote and sent the following email off to her old employer.

Dear Prime Minister,

I was your justice adviser in the Policy Advisory Group for a few months in 2010.

Shortly after leaving the Department of the Prime Minister and Cabinet, I was diagnosed with terminal brain cancer.

I am writing to let you know that I am filing High Court proceedings later today against the attorney-general for a declaration that the Crimes Act 1961, when interpreted consistently with the New Zealand Bill of Rights Act 1990, does not make physician-assisted dying illegal for those who have an irremediable medical condition and are suffering intolerably. A recent judgment of the full Canadian

Supreme Court gives me cause to think I may be successful.

Alternatively, my counsel, Andrew Butler, will advocate for a declaration that the relevant Crimes Act provisions are inconsistent with the Bill of Rights Act. The courts have never made a declaration of inconsistency before, but this could be the first one!

I wanted to forewarn you, as there is likely to be media interest in the case.

Kind regards,
Lecretia Seales

As Lecretia was preparing to file her statement of claim, I was preparing to return to Vancouver for a week to resume my leadership course. As I boarded my flight, a lawyer from Russell McVeagh was walking down Lambton Quay to deliver documents to the High Court in Wellington, and Cate was sending our press release out far and wide. On the plane I picked at airline food and watched movies, stories about superheroes and wronged men and dystopian futures. I couldn't sleep. I sensed something big was about to happen. And Lecretia, my incredible wife, was compelling me to step up, to change in ways I'd never expected, so that I could be the husband she needed me to be for whatever came next.

Chapter 17

IN VANCOUVER, WHILE I waited in the long line to clear passport control, I turned on my phone for the first time in fourteen hours and glanced at the screen. Notifications fired in from multiple sources: emails, Twitter, Facebook, and other applications long since forgotten.

Lecretia's face was on the front page of every major newspaper in the country. The two major television networks were running stories. The radio stations were expanding on the news at every hourly bulletin. Lecretia was suddenly famous: for being terminally ill, for wanting to have a choice about how she died, for taking her case to the High Court.

It was a strange feeling. Lecretia had always been an

advocate for law reform and someone who had debated for justice for others. But in filing her statement of claim, Lecretia had become an actor, not merely an advocate, and she was centre stage. She would be judged, her motivations questioned, her ideas challenged. My wife and her circumstances had become a national talking point, and everyone had an opinion. John Key had not replied to Lecretia's email, but he now authorised a statement to the media: 'The prime minister is aware of Ms Seales' illness and his thoughts are with her at this difficult time.'

In late March I returned from Canada and was reunited with Lecretia. I was excited to see her. I embraced her and kissed her as though I'd been away for much longer. I was proud of what she had done. She was happy too, and looking forward to the court case. The team at Russell McVeagh had begun assembling evidence from experts all over the world and preparing Lecretia's affidavits.

But I was shocked by her decline. She was walking nowhere near as well as when I left her, just a week earlier, and her speech had taken on a slur. Her left hand hung uselessly at her side. But if the changes were obvious to me, they did not appear to be obvious to her, as her humour and spirit remained undiminished. If she knew that her health was deteriorating, she wasn't letting on.

As the case drew closer, I wondered whether she was up to the challenge she had set herself. I was still unsure about Andrew Butler too. As a Catholic, could he suspend his beliefs and run this case? My question, which I posed to Tim Clarke, partner at Russell McVeagh, was a simple one.

'Is Andrew more Catholic than lawyer?'

A lawyer's job, Tim explained, is not to agree or disagree with the client but to mount the best case possible on the client's behalf. What Andrew believed was irrelevant: his job was to advocate, to speak for Lecretia, and not to advance his own agenda. It was fascinating, but the contradiction between what Lecretia wanted and what Andrew's faith taught and believed was a source of concern for me.

Then I thought about Christopher Finlayson, the New Zealand attorney-general, the man Lecretia was symbolically taking to court as the Crown's representative. The man was a devout Catholic, but also gay. He has been reported as describing himself as an 'odd fish'. Clearly some Catholics were comfortable living with contradiction and balancing the demands of their faith with the real world. Maybe Andrew was capable of this too.

As Lecretia engaged more with the media, she strived to remain as neutral as possible, siding with no political party, as the issue of assisted dying, based on the polls we'd seen, had broad popular support. The Labour Party had been more active in advocating for assisted dying in the past, but the National Party was now in power with twice the support of its rival and no change would happen without them. If we made it a National issue or a Labour issue, people might turn against it, whether they believed in it or not. Although Labour and National had been fighting over the centre for decades and there was no longer much discernible difference between them, there was still a lingering tribalism among their supporters.

Lecretia and I went home to Tauranga for Easter for Lecretia's forty-second birthday. Her brother Jeremy, now in Auckland, came down for the weekend with his wife, Kate, and son, Rafferty. Kat and her new husband, Andrew, also joined us. Lecretia had resumed chemotherapy a few days prior, and it was knocking her around. She spent a lot of time resting on her parents' couch at their home, without saying much. She smiled when four-year-old Rafferty entered the room, but he was now a little scared of his aunt, whose physical decline was becoming more obvious. It must have broken Lecretia's heart. She would have dearly loved to scoop him up in a hug and hold him to her.

That weekend I wrote my first post for Lecretia's blog, describing our weekend in Tauranga together. I published it and monitored the traffic in real time as it circulated through the social media networks. The issue was touching people. Michael Laws, former Labour MP, and architect of the first assisted-dying bill in 1995, made supportive comments on Lecretia's Facebook page, along with Don Brash, the former National Party leader. Helen Kelly, a staunch left-wing employee rights advocate who ran the Council of Trade Unions, suffering from terminal cancer herself, publicly shared her support. Right-wing blogger David Farrar backed Lecretia's efforts on his blog. Chris Trotter, a left-wing political commentator, wrote a long endorsement of Lecretia's legal challenge, calling her 'brave and deeply ethical'. Other comments were made by Jackie Blue, a former National MP, and Lianne Dalziel, a former Labour MP and now mayor of Christchurch. It was truly an issue that crossed political boundaries. It boiled down to one essential question: what rights does an individual have to choose?

Opposition to Lecretia's campaign was mobilising too. Shortly after the statement of claim was filed, a group called the Care Alliance declared their intention to intervene in the case. The Care Alliance was made up of palliative care groups (Hospice New Zealand, the Australian and New Zealand Society of Palliative Medicine, the New Zealand Health Professionals Alliance, and Palliative Care Nurses

New Zealand), Christian groups (Lutherans for Life, the Salvation Army, the Nathaniel Centre, and the Christian Medical Fellowship), and lobby groups (Family First New Zealand, a politically organised anti-progressive movement founded by a former Christian radio broadcaster, Bob McCoskrie; Euthanasia-Free NZ, a purportedly secular group that ran many fear-mongering events in Catholic venues; and Not Dead Yet Aotearoa, a disability rights group that had its roots in the United States).

The Care Alliance claimed it represented both faith-based and secular groups, but it was not hard to see its conservative Christian streak. Both hospices and palliative care have their roots in religion, and the leadership of hospices today tends to be assumed by people of faith. The proportion of practising Christians in palliative care and hospice care is far higher than in any other area of medicine—demonstrably true in Australia, anecdotally true in New Zealand. In fact, much of the practice around our end-of-life care is rooted in the application of dogmatic Christian values, whether those same values are held by the patient or not.

Though Lecretia was annoyed by the intervention, it wasn't unexpected. There had been similar challenges in Canada and in other cases overseas. While neither of us was a Christian in the churchgoing sense, Lecretia and I both sought a relationship with the divine that was personal and unfiltered through organised religion. We believed in good and evil, but we both believed that context meant everything. A dying patient seeking mercy is very different from a patient being put to death against their will—but as we saw it, the law and the Christian values that underpinned it did not reflect that subtlety, a subtlety we believed that a merciful God was more than capable of.

As a child Lecretia attended a Baptist church in Tauranga, and she enjoyed Sunday school, I suspect more for the singing and the stories than anything else. But she was instilled with a faith in and respect for God. She drifted away from Baptism in her teenage years, but some vestige of faith remained. For Lecretia, that meant a private spirituality and the practice of kindness and generosity. She put others first, not in the hope of any eternal reward, but just because it felt like the right thing to do. I think Lecretia saw the source of that motivation as God, and felt that the same impulse was present in her fellow human beings. It didn't come from fear—it came from respect for others. A person's evil acts could generally, she thought, be traced to evil done to them—cycles of abuse, poverty, cruelty. She believed that kindness and compassion were a sort of universal solvent—applied liberally, they could melt any twisted mesh of evil.

While Lecretia was tolerant of others' religious beliefs, and a spiritual person, I am less so. If I am spiritual at all, it's in my gratitude for being alive, witness to the spectacular confluence of chance and history that is life. To me, if God is anything, it abides in the infinite six that follows the decimal point in the odds of one side of a cosmic die. God is in the mathematical probability of one event happening and not another. Its motives are inscrutable and its attitude to humanity indifferent. We all live under a rain of infinite possibilities beyond our control, and our free will is the flimsy umbrella that shelters us from a deluge of pure chance. And for that reason alone—that common destiny of being at the mercy of fate—we have no excuse to be anything other than kind to one another. Sooner or later, it is our number that is up, and we rely on others to help us bear that burden.

I placed my trust in science, but Lecretia preferred to follow her instincts. I remember discussing Darwin's theory of evolution with her once, that all life came from pre-cellular molecules, then cells, then specialised cells, then aggregations of complementary cells and so on, ultimately culminating in animals, and then higher-order beings like us.

'I don't believe any of that.'

'But it's science.'

'I don't care.'

'There are experiments that prove a lot of this.'

'It's so boring, and it doesn't matter.'

Lecretia was not interested in science at all—and had avoided it through her schooling, preferring to focus on classics and literature and languages. For her the assertions of scientists were indistinguishable from those of religious leaders, and could be dismissed or accepted according to some internal barometer of truth.

Lecretia and I both felt that the members of the Care Alliance were ignoring their own internal barometers. We, and most New Zealanders, agreed that if a person is in pain, with no hope of recovery, then they should be able to ask for help to die and have someone help them. It was logical and it felt right. It was free will at work. But it seemed to me that the Care Alliance believed a patient's ongoing suffering was justified, no matter how bad—upholding the existing law was more important to them than doing what felt right for most people.

When Lecretia announced her statement of claim, the Care Alliance was quick to condemn her actions. Family First claimed her case 'should not be solved in the courtroom'. That was, of course, completely wrong: the law had to be tested in the courts. Where else could it be tested, and what else could she do? The truth was

Family First feared and opposed change in conflict with its religious beliefs.

The Care Alliance was not the only organisation to get involved in Lecretia's case. Countering it was the Voluntary Euthanasia Society of New Zealand, a group of mostly elderly people who campaigned for choices at the end of life. They saw a place for voluntary assisted dying for patients with Alzheimer's and other degenerative illnesses in those cases where an advance directive had been put in place expressing the individual's wishes ahead of time. The group was led by a retired intensive care medical specialist, Dr Jack Havill, and counted among its allies the former Labour MP Maryan Street.

Also asking to participate was the Human Rights Commission, an independent crown entity not answerable to the government. Its motivation was to provide expertise in the interpretation of the bill of rights, and it sought to join the case on a neutral basis.

After Easter, I went home to Wellington so I could return to work, while Lecretia stayed in Tauranga with her parents. She finally took leave from her own job at the Law Commission, ostensibly to focus on the case, but the truth was that she was exhausted. Unless Lecretia's condition improved, she wasn't going to return to work.

We discussed her resigning a few times, so that she could focus on her health, but she refused. She also had a gym membership that she wouldn't cancel, as she intended to get back to the gym as soon as she was able. Between bouts of nausea and drowsiness, she continued making inquiries about a trip to India. She wanted to go to a tiger game-park and see the Taj Mahal.

Lecretia had not given up. If she said goodbye to her job, and the gym, that would have been saying that she no longer expected to return to them. Lecretia's very life was all about her work—she loved law reform, and she didn't know what she would do with herself otherwise. In the end, I convinced her that perhaps the Law Commission would allow her to take a longer period of unpaid leave. They could hold her position open, and she could retain her office on the nineteenth floor with its spectacular views of Wellington Harbour. As soon as the hearing was done, if she was well enough, she could return. She agreed to this, and finished work—temporarily, in her view.

Lecretia's first TV interview was with the journalist Emma Alberici, on the Australian Broadcasting Corporation's current affairs program *Lateline*. It went to air on 10 April 2015. The ABC crew travelled to Tauranga to Shirley and Larry's home to mic Lecretia up and put her on camera. We felt that if we could bring international attention to Lecretia's plight, it might act as a catalyst for the domestic campaign. Despite not being able to see Ms Alberici, and only being able to hear her questions through an earpiece, Lecretia was lucid and assured throughout the interview. She did a great job. She showed passion and humour, and I was proud of her. The hair loss, the paralysis of the left-hand side of her face and the slightly slurred words were on display, but she made her points clearly and intelligently. Her beauty shone through.

Though I had returned to work in Wellington, running Lecretia's campaign was getting to be a full-time job. I had to write blog posts, engage on social media, and review the applications from the interveners and our lawyers' responses so I could keep Lecretia up to date. Shirley called me from Tauranga, where Lecretia still was, and told me that Lecretia's illness now required constant attention, as she needed help to move around, to be fed, to be taken to the bathroom. And she needed company. I couldn't bear the idea of not being with her any more, and I spoke to Xero about this in mid-April. It was agreed that I would take indefinite leave, which was a huge relief. In January I'd recently been appointed the global head and vice-president of bank integration, a lofty title for the job I'd largely been doing anyway, but my new position brought with it higher expectations, and it was hard to see how I could do any justice to this role while caring for my wife when she returned home from Tauranga. I had drinks with my workmates on my last day, a lot of them now firm friends, and knew I would miss them. I didn't know when I would be back.

Chapter 18

THE HIGH COURT was scheduled to hear the applications to intervene in Lecretia's case in late April in Wellington. Though Lecretia was still in Tauranga, we spoke nearly every day. Tauranga was experiencing a late summer, so a lot of her afternoons were spent on her parents' deck, eating feijoas from a tree in her mother's garden, or cherries from a local orchard. When I was on a FaceTime call with her I would scoop up Ferdinand, so that she could see him, and talk to him.

On 21 April I went along to the High Court to hear the interveners—the parties that wanted to be involved in the hearing—make their case to be included. The judge would need to decide whether to include the interveners before the hearing started in May. I entered the courtroom and sat in the public gallery, looking out at the courtroom floor, where the various counsels had assembled in groups. I saw Andrew Butler for the first time, and Chris Curran, and I liked them immediately. They were young, and dynamic, and passionate, and I could tell they were really keen to get into the case. I also saw those acting for the attorney-general, and the interveners too. The attorney-general was represented by Michael Heron, the solicitor-general, who wasn't present, and Paul Rishworth QC, an imperious-looking man who spoke with the creaky voice of the pages of long-forgotten legal tomes. If he was excited by the prospect of the case, he didn't show it. The Care Alliance was represented by Victoria Casey, a woman with curly grey hair and a serious expression. As a board member of the archdiocese of Wellington, she had strong ties to the Catholic Church. The Voluntary Euthanasia Society was represented by Kate Davenport QC, who seemed relaxed and good-humoured. And the Human Rights Commission was represented by Matthew Palmer QC, Geoffrey Palmer's son, a successful lawyer in his own right, who shared his father's rake-thin height and friendly features.

After a few minutes, the bailiff announced the judge was about to enter the courtroom and called for those present to rise. The judge entered the room and invited the court to take a seat. Justice David Collins was grey-haired, with an open, likeable face. He looked like someone capable of both kindness and sternness. He had a reputation for being firm but fair. When it was announced that he would be presiding over Lecretia's case, we were pleased. The High Court judiciary were reputed to be almost uniformly conservative, but Justice Collins was regarded as someone who was at least capable of having an open mind.

Andrew Butler was one of the first to speak, and made the point that Lecretia's case was really about her own circumstances, not broader society, and therefore the judge should not grant any of the applicants leave to intervene. The broader debate should happen after the court case, in the public arena and in parliament. Besides which, for Lecretia, time was of the essence, and the risk of the interveners filibustering the case was too great. He also pointed out that if the Care Alliance had evidence it thought relevant, that evidence could be put forward by the Crown's counsel.

Justice Collins then asked to hear from the Care Alliance. As if to prove Andrew Butler's point about wasting Lecretia's time, Ms Casey launched into a long and emotive argument for the Care Alliance's participation. She advanced and circled and backtracked, speculating about the effects of assisted dying on the elderly and disabled, about the troublesome decisions made in overseas jurisdictions, about the precedent that would be set, about slippery slopes and the thin ends of wedges and more.

Justice Collins called for a recess halfway through her monologue, and I had a coffee with Andrew and Chris.

'We have a great case,' Andrew said. 'The evidence that Catherine Marks and the team have assembled is excellent. The defence has little to support their case. If they win, it'll be because of the inadequacy of the law, not because what Lecretia wants is wrong or dangerous. We've looked, and there's no compelling evidence not to allow Lecretia to have what she wants.'

Catherine had begun gathering expert testimony from witnesses around the globe who had worked in jurisdictions that allowed assisted dying. She had spoken to doctors, ethicists and professors about their experiences, and the conversations were revealing: assisted dying was helping patients manage their suffering and live longer lives.

'I apologise if this is a rude question, Andrew, but aren't you Catholic?' I said.

'I am,' he said, 'but having reviewed the evidence I'm genuinely of the view that assisted dying in circumstances like Lecretia's is justified—and this case is about Lecretia's circumstances only. The Care Alliance has no real cause to intervene.'

'Wouldn't it set a precedent, though?'

'The ruling would only apply to Lecretia. Anyone else who sought assisted dying consequently would need to go through the courts. It would open a pathway, but the courts would remain gatekeepers to its use.'

We returned to the courtroom, and Victoria Casey resumed speaking about the effects of assisted dying on the vulnerable and the elderly and the disabled, speculating on how people might be coerced, how no process is safe. She was speaking from the same playbook anti-assisted-dying campaigners relied on the world over. Justice Lynn Smith in the Canadian courts had examined all of these claims, and in her extensive review of the evidence, she found them all wanting. The things people feared—suicide contagion, elderly relatives and the disabled being bumped off against their will, the dissolution of the doctor–patient relationship—they were just not happening.

The Care Alliance had perhaps taken their cue from American Wesley J. Smith, one of the world's foremost anti-assisted-dying campaigners, who argued that the best way to fight assisted dying—regardless of one's own religious beliefs—was to make secular arguments. His view was that faith-based arguments were not generally successful—and particularly not in secular institutions such as courts. His views were extremely influential, and not just in the United States. When you look at the various anti-assisted-dying campaigns around the world today, God is not usually part of the discussion, though the Catholic idea of sanctity of life might be.

Casey finally finished some time after lunch. The other applicants, from the Voluntary Euthanasia Society and the Human Rights Commission, were mercifully brief. The hearing ended at 4 pm, and I went to the airport to collect Lecretia and her mother, Shirley. It was good to see them both, but Lecretia's physical transformation was clearly more advanced. Her left eye was slightly bulging from the swelling, and her left hand was now completely paralysed, curled up against her body like a talon. She was still walking but only just. Her first item of business when we arrived home was to greet Ferdinand. She cooed at him, and let his fur brush her cheek.

I explained what had happened at the High Court, and described Andrew's opening statements, and Victoria Casey's longwinded arguments. She sighed in frustration at the suggestion she was vulnerable, and that she didn't know what she was asking for or its implications. Russell

McVeagh had prepared some affidavits for Lecretia to sign based on prior interviews they had conducted with her, and I read these to her. She listened and nodded, interjecting occasionally.

Lecretia had agreed to only one big interview, with Television New Zealand's weekly in-depth current affairs program, *Sunday*. On Tuesday 21 April, the team arrived in Wellington. Lecretia would be interviewed by Janet McIntyre, one of the country's most incisive television journalists.

The cameraman took his first shots of Lecretia and me walking along Wellington's Lambton Quay towards the Law Commission. We went inside and Lecretia went to her office, where she immediately began checking her emails and going through the papers on her desk. It was the first time she'd been in the office since Easter. Lecretia took a file box and balanced it over her useless left arm as she carried it to her desk. She ignored the cameraman as she caught up with her work.

On Wednesday, a studio was set up in our lounge, and Lecretia and Janet had their first long conversation. Lecretia was calm and assured, laying out her reasons for pursuing the case. As I watched her speak, I noticed how the room fell silent. My wife had taken on a new quality—*mana*—speaking with a self-assurance and dignity approaching that of a Māori kaumātua, secure in her wisdom. She'd always had grace, and presence, but this was something else. There was alchemy in the room. As Lecretia unburdened her secrets, and her fears, she displayed a vulnerability I had not seen before, and that willingness to be vulnerable gave her a stronger voice.

The producer wanted me to be in the story, but I hadn't made up my mind. I thought back to the conversation I'd had with Lecretia in Kaikoura, the fear that people might see me as the instigator of all this, the dark svengali whispering in my lover's ear. In the end the charm of Janet and her colleagues and the respect with which they were treating Lecretia won me over. The next day, Lecretia and I were interviewed together. It was my favourite part of the shoot. We talked about our marriage, and our struggles with fertility. Lecretia was whip-smart, as always, but good-humoured too, quick to correct my spotty memory but laughing as she did so.

Janet's questions turned to Lecretia's terminal diagnosis and her decline, and what we would do if it all became too much. At the time, Lecretia was drafting an advance directive setting out her wishes. She did not want artificial feeding, did not want her breathing sustained. If she was dying, she was to be left to die. But in that advance directive was a special clause: in the event that she became

mentally incompetent, I would have power of attorney—
if permitted by law or judicial ruling—to instruct a doctor
to end her life. Janet pressed me on that point. How did I
feel about that?

I answered honestly.

'I don't know. It's probably fair to say not many people
will have experienced that, so there's not a lot to go on.'

'This is actually giving you the right to say, this is it,
it's over.'

'Yes.'

'Giving a doctor permission to end your wife's life.'

'Yes. Well, it's the fulfilment of her wishes. It's the
wishes that she'd set out and made clear in a state of mental
competence. If I had any doubt that it was not what she
wanted, I wouldn't be able to follow it through. But she
has been very clear that this is what she wants.' I turned to
Lecretia. 'Haven't you?'

'Yes,' Lecretia replied. 'And I do not want you to have
a mad wife to look after.'

'Really?' asked Janet.

'Yes,' she said, smiling. 'If I am mad, then I have
already died, in my own mind.'

'Look,' I said, 'the decision is ultimately going to be:
is my wife suffering? Is my wife suffering, and can I see
that she's suffering? Is there any hope that she won't suffer,

is there any hope that she'll come back to me?' I spoke slowly, searching for the words. 'When that's clear, then I would be compelled to follow her wishes, and to instruct the doctor to proceed with what she'd decided.'

Lecretia listened quietly when I spoke, silently agreeing with what I said. If she'd objected, she would have said so. When I'd misdescribed her wedding dress in an earlier part of the interview, she was quick to correct me. There's no doubt she would have corrected me on this.

Later that afternoon, there was some filming in town at Lecretia's favourite café, a Parisian-style salon de thé called Louis Sergeant, where they served herbal teas and the most spectacular cakes I'd ever seen. When Lecretia was still working, she used to schedule lunch dates there with friends, and held court while catching up on news. But on this day she was being filmed with her mother, beneath a large portrait of Marie Antoinette. A couple of desserts were served.

'What's this, Lecretia?' asked Shirley.

'That's the L'Intense. It's chocolate and it's got peanut and salted caramel in the base. It's my favourite.'

Without any warning she cried out and tipped sideways out of her chair onto the floor of the café, almost taking the table and the desserts with her. Thankfully she didn't hit her head. She had just lost her balance. But it was another reminder of how fragile she was. There was such a disconnect between the strength of her spirit and the failure of her body.

As Lecretia was helped back up, all she said was, 'How embarrassing.'

And then she got on with enjoying her dessert.

On Friday we went to see the oncologist. We were still hopeful. There had to be something. Lecretia still had her fighting spirit, and so much to live for.

But the oncologist did not see any point in Lecretia continuing with chemotherapy. Her movements were weakening rapidly. He said it was time to consider palliative care. She should be speaking with a hospice.

We knew what that meant. Lecretia was dying.

I couldn't accept it.

'We have to try something. Are there clinical trials, new overseas treatments? Immunotherapy?'

He gave us a few leads, but everything now was a long shot. I asked him to give her a new prescription for temozolomide. It was the only drug that had had any noticeable effect. The secondary chemotherapy had at best slowed things down, and at worst had no effect at all. Temozolomide had at least got Lecretia walking without a stick again, and feeling good.

Unfortunately Lecretia's platelet count was down again, so he wouldn't prescribe it. But he gave us hope by saying that, if things improved, he could prescribe it again later. In the meantime, he gave us some phone numbers for palliative care teams. He said it wasn't too early to talk to them, as they could make Lecretia more comfortable around the house.

Lecretia seemed unmoved by the news, as if she was expecting it. Shirley and I were devastated. We drove home.

The team from *Sunday* wanted to do another interview that afternoon before they returned to Auckland, but I wasn't sure.

'They want to come over,' I said. 'Do we want them to?'

'They can come over,' said Lecretia. 'They may as well.'

'Are you sure?'

'Yes.'

The team showed up shortly after lunch. They decided to do another interview, this time with Lecretia and her mother. It was a lovely interview, and it came out, finally, that Lecretia had been justice adviser to John Key, at the Department of the Prime Minister and Cabinet. This piqued Janet's interest.

'What did you think of the job?'

Lecretia's eyes sparkled. 'I found it really exciting. I loved knowing what was going on behind closed doors.'

'And what was your relationship to Prime Minister John Key?'

'I was his adviser, so I would give him regular briefing notes advising him on choices to be made in the justice sector.'

'What did the prime minister make of your advice?'

'It was generally accepted.'

'How did you find this work?'

She smiled broadly, the left side of her mouth sagging only slightly. 'Really exciting. Really exciting. And I guess I would know if my advice was taken or not, judging from the cabinet minutes as to what actually happened in cabinet.'

'Any comments to make on the prime minister himself? Did you have any dealings with him?'

'Yes, I really liked him. I did have a few dealings with the prime minister, and he was a very easy man to get along with, and he was hard not to like.'

'Would you have a message for him, at the moment?'

She paused, thinking carefully, her longest pause of the day so far.

'Please don't put end-of-life issues on the backburner. It's a really important issue, and as our population ages it's going to become more and more important. So please deal with it. Please deal with it and don't shy away from it, because actually, it is popular.'

'What specifically would you like him to take up and do?'

'I would like to see legislation that clarifies a process for enabling physician-assisted dying for terminally ill patients.'

'Why do you think there's reluctance to take this up?'

'There are divided opinions on it. But actually the polls have shown the vast majority of New Zealanders support some form of dying with dignity.'

'Shirley, just listening to that, what do you think of your little girl?'

Shirley smiled, as Lecretia sat beside her and listened. 'She's making me proud, just like she always has.'

'Do you think she has it in her, to make a change?'

'If anybody can do it, she can. And when she first told us about what she was going to do, her eyes lit up, and I could see the passion burning there to make a difference. And for that alone I'd support her.'

'The very fact that she's doing it, at a time when she's facing pain and suffering, is astounding,' said Janet.

'It is astounding. She might make history.'

'Is that what you want, Lecretia?'

'I want to make things easier for people coming after me,' Lecretia told her. 'I want to make a difference to the law. And it's quite exciting that I'm in a position where I might be able to do that.'

She had just learned that chemotherapy was no longer an option. Her excitement and motivation amazed me. Where did my wife get her strength from? On the back deck, where she was being filmed, in the sunlight, she looked luminous. I adored her.

I realised that Lecretia had decided, somewhere deep inside her, that she would not be cancer's victim. She would make every day count. If she suffered, but the law changed, it meant others would not needlessly suffer. With the cancer taking everything from her—her hope of children, her career, and her future—she had still found a purpose, one that was consistent with her calling as a reformer of the law.

With the final interview done, the *Sunday* team packed up their gear and left.

Later that day the phone rang. It was Catherine Marks.

'I've got some bad news,' she said. 'The interveners were successful. But there are limitations on how they can participate. They can submit written evidence only on particular areas. It's not clear if they'll get to speak at the hearing. I'll send you the judgment through.'

I reviewed the document. The Care Alliance was able to present evidence on how Lecretia's case might affect the disabled community. Nothing else. And their written submission was limited to 6000 words. The good news, I surmised, was that the Care Alliance couldn't claim their voices were going to be excluded. If we won, they couldn't protest that they had not been allowed to participate. The date was confirmed, and the hearing was due to begin in four weeks' time.

Chapter 19

ON 29 APRIL, we had our first appointment with the palliative care team, who came to our home to meet Lecretia, and to assess what she needed. They were aware of her High Court case, but didn't tell us their thoughts on it. They treated Lecretia like any other patient.

She was given a wheelchair, and an electric armchair that tilted upwards so that she could get into a standing position from a seated one. She was given a walking frame too, but couldn't use it, because her left arm couldn't hold the frame properly. We gave them a copy of Lecretia's advance directive, so that they'd know her wishes if she suddenly got ill. No artificial feeding or breathing, maximum pain relief, and the clause she inserted that said she could be helped to die if she reached a state of mental incompetence and the judge ruled it permissible. We felt she was still a long way from that point, but it seemed like the right thing for her to set that out clearly while she was still able.

On that day, we learned that in South Africa a lawyer named Robin Stransham-Ford, who was suffering from prostate cancer, had won a case in the High Court in Pretoria for the right to be assisted by a doctor to die. Stransham-Ford had been supported by DignitySA, the organisation formed by Sean Davison, the professor convicted of helping his mother to die in New Zealand in 2006.

In summarising the evidence, the judge in Stransham-Ford's case said:

> The common-law crimes of murder or culpable homicide in the context of assisted suicide by medical practitioners, insofar as they provide for an absolute prohibition, unjustifiably limit the applicant's constitutional rights to human dignity, and freedom to bodily and psychological integrity, and to that extent are declared to be overbroad and in conflict with the said provisions of the bill of rights.

Mr Stransham-Ford was victorious, and instantly became a hero to many people around the world, including Lecretia.

This was exactly the outcome we were hoping to achieve in New Zealand: the South African judge had found conflict between his country's existing laws and its bill of rights. It was a brave, compassionate, and forceful judgment.

Lecretia's legal team had begun the task of preparing evidentiary affidavits. Before the hearing began, every party to the case was given time to assemble their evidence. The evidence took the form of written testimonies from expert witnesses, each sworn to be true by their author and compiled by lawyers. Our affidavits were due first, then the interveners would provide theirs, before the Crown would file its own. Copies were distributed to all parties in the case at the same time as they were submitted to the High Court. We would have a chance to provide reply affidavits to the evidence that the Crown and interveners had presented. At the hearing itself, the plaintiff and defendant would make their case before the judge in the form of an oral argument, referring back to the points made and the facts declared in the affidavits.

Lecretia submitted two affidavits in her own name. She outlined her circumstances, her background, and her reasons for making her claim. She asserted that she had not been coerced, that she was not vulnerable, that she enjoyed her life and valued it, and that she was competent enough to make decisions about how and when her life should end.

She described the cruel choice she faced: take her own life early, while she could, or face the prospect of a lingering death. She described the likely progression of her disease, and how she feared it might rob her of all dignity in her last weeks, or even months. She should be the one to decide when the indignity was too great to suffer. This was a personal question, she said, and no one else should be able to answer it for her. If she could choose to die with the help of her doctor, she could live as long as she still wanted to—much longer than if she had to take her life on her own. This freedom to choose would itself be palliative: she would no longer be anxious, the victim of her illness, worried about what might happen to her, but the architect and arbiter of her life, and her death.

The progression of her illness was affirmed by her GP, and her oncologist. Her oncologist said she had less than twelve months to live, and her disease was incurable. Her GP was willing to prescribe or administer life-ending medication if Lecretia wanted this to happen.

This was important, because it was evidence that there were general practitioners in New Zealand who believed in assisted dying for the terminally ill. Plenty of doctors had gone on the record over the years saying that helping a patient to die is unethical; it was up to us to prove that this view was not universal. The fact that Lecretia's GP had treated her for years, long before she was ill, helped our case. Lecretia hadn't gone shopping for a doctor who would back her up—and what were the chances that she was already seeing the only GP in the country prepared to do this? If her GP was willing to testify as such in an affidavit, there were certainly others in the country who would do the same.

Dr Libby Smales, a retired palliative care physician from Hawkes Bay, testified that she had encountered many patients throughout her career who had expressed a wish to die. She told the story of a desperate man who had driven his mobility scooter off a cliff to avoid the torment of the final stages of motor neurone disease. He did not die, and the fall compounded his problems, making his death worse than it ought to have been. She had also seen a fiercely independent woman, suffering from arterial insufficiency and intractable pain in her old age, choose to starve herself to death rather than face the eventual amputation of both her legs. With assisted dying, she might have lived longer. Dr Smales talked about the many benefits of palliative care, but also testified to its limits, particularly for independent people like Lecretia.

Dr Michael Ashby, a respected palliative care professor and former president of the Australian and New Zealand Society of Palliative Medicine, made a similar argument, testifying that palliative care, though a good thing, has limitations, just as medicine does. He estimated that between 10 and 20 per cent of patients who enter hospice care say at some point that they wish to die faster, but less than 5 per cent express such a wish consistently, over an extended period. He said that someone like Lecretia— independent, intellectual, active—was likely to be among that 5 per cent. Like Libby Smales, Dr Ashby said he knew of terminally ill people who had taken their lives early. These patients were not depressed, but wanted to truncate the dying process, and had chosen to overdose on medication while they were still able to do so unaided. He then spoke specifically about Lecretia's case, and described the risk of coning, explaining that the brain would herniate down into the spinal canal, putting pressure on the brain stem, likely requiring her to be terminally sedated. Terminal sedation is the act of providing pain medication and sedatives to a dying patient to put them to sleep and withholding food and fluids until they starve to death. Lecretia was clear: she did not want to linger on, half alive, sedated until she starved. That was not what she regarded as a good death.

Other experts concurred in their affidavits that palliative care was not necessarily the best option for every patient, and that it had to be judged on a case-by-case basis. Dr Rajesh Munglani, a consultant in pain medicine, talked about the limitations of pain relief, and how advanced cancer, like Lecretia's, can be unresponsive to palliation. He said she might ultimately be forced to choose death by suicide, like many others in her circumstances, or face unbearable pain and consequent sedation. Professor Owens, an expert in palliative psychology from the University of Auckland, asserted that someone with Lecretia's personality, which he described as driven and perfectionist, might not respond well to palliative care. Both Dr Munglani and Professor Owens had over thirty years' experience in their respective fields.

Professor Owens also made reference to a discussion published in the *Journal of the American Medical Association* by Drs Orentlicher, Rich and Mason that drew a distinction between committing suicide, which results from impaired thinking, and making a rational decision to die, which does not. A psychologist who deals with suicidal patients tries to help them understand their symptoms are treatable. When a patient is both mentally competent and terminally ill, and makes a rational decision to die, that approach is not appropriate—the condition underlying the symptoms isn't treatable, and it would be disingenuous to say it was. Professor Owens noted that suicidal patients who are prevented from dying often go on to enjoy long and happy lives, while a terminally ill person who makes a conscious, rational decision to die but is not permitted to do so lives only a short time longer anyway, and suffers physically and psychologically as a result. He noted too that suicide tends to tear families apart, whereas the families of those who make a conscious, rational decision to die are often brought together, and may find it easier to deal with their grief. The affidavit of Frank Spring, made on behalf of the New Mexico Psychological Association, drew a similar distinction between committing suicide and seeking help to die, describing them as 'fundamentally different psychological phenomena'. He asserted that these two categories of patients must be treated differently by the law, so that the terminally ill could receive adequate psychological support at the end of their lives.

There were also affidavits from two retired GPs from Oregon, Dr David Grube and Dr Peter Reagan, who had over seventy years of experience between them. Dr Reagan was the first doctor to write a prescription of life-ending drugs under Oregon law. Dr Grube, in the eighteen years that assisted dying had been legal in Oregon, had only prescribed the drugs thirty times, and almost always to patients he knew very well and had known for a long time. He would only prescribe after discussing all other options with his patients, including possible treatments, palliative care, or doing nothing, and would discuss these over a period of months. He described his experience of prescribing life-ending medication to patients, and how without exception it was an enormous relief to them, whether or not they ultimately went on to use it—a point also made by Professor Owens, who cited evidence to support this view.

Dr Phillipa Malpas, a senior lecturer in psychological medicine at Auckland University, told the story of a woman named Gloria who had suffered cardiovascular disease. Rather than endure a drawn-out death through her illness, she decided to dehydrate herself. 'If I'd had Nembutal in my cupboard,' Gloria said to Dr Malpas in her final days, 'it might have given me a little more time. That is the key. If you know there is a way out, you can focus on what life has to offer. You can balance the pain and suffering because if it gets to that point, you can end it.' Gloria died after enduring nine days of dehydration.

Another witness, whose name was suppressed, testified with a personal story about his wife, who was dying of a rare case of melanoma on her brain and spinal cord. It was a tremendously painful illness, unresponsive to medication. She had spent eight months of her life paralysed and incontinent. She hated morphine as it put her in a stupor. She had much to live for but she was unmistakably dying. While she was able, and before she was paralysed, she bought Nembutal online, risking prosecution. 'Once she had the Nembutal in her possession,' said the witness, 'she stopped focusing on dying and began to focus on living again.' Ultimately, after months of being paralysed and incontinent, she decided that the time had come for her to take the drug. She did, and died peacefully. Her husband, though shattered by grief, was glad she hadn't suffered more than she was willing to bear. He did not see his wife as a suicide—the very word was offensive to him—but as someone who lived with a fatal illness, and refused to be its victim. Not only did his wife not have to endure more than she was able, he did not have to deal with the grief of her taking her own life violently, or watching her in agony until she drew her last breath. It was what she wanted.

Reading these affidavits and discussing them together clarified our thinking. We both believed that, like murder, suicide is wrong. The taking of another's life is the worst of all crimes, and the taking of one's own life is the worst of all tragedies. Like most New Zealanders, both Lecretia and I had experienced the great sadness that comes from knowing people who take their own lives too soon. Lecretia and her high school girlfriends lost three boys they were close to in a spate of suicides in the 1980s, and she saw the terrible impact their deaths had on their families and friends—but not all self-elected deaths should be regarded as suicide.

A good example is the tragedy of 9/11. In the doomed towers, the innocent office workers faced a terrible choice: perish in the flames or fall to their deaths. To the moral absolutist, those who chose the first were victims of murder, and those who chose the second were suicides. To the human being, there is no such distinction—only the choice between a slow painful death or a quick, violent one. When death is inevitable, that is the only choice that has any importance. The chief New York medical examiner, Charles Hirsch, thought so too. He refused to classify the people who had jumped to their deaths as suicides or 'jumpers'. They were victims of terrorism. No sane person would call those people suicides for taking their own lives in that situation. How can we look at a dying person who wants to make a choice about how they die, and condemn them for wanting to minimise their own suffering? Is it always suicide when you take your own life? Is it always murder when you take another's? Are there degrees of murder and suicide? Courts were already grappling with these distinctions, and in New Zealand Lecretia intended to force the issue. Lecretia's illness was her burning building.

We knew we were on the right side of the debate. All the examples of palliative care working in patients' interests didn't mitigate the examples where it didn't or couldn't. People were suffering against their will, and assisted-dying legislation had the potential to bring those people some relief.

The next affidavits submitted to the High Court were those of the interveners: the Care Alliance, arguing against us, and the Voluntary Euthanasia Society, who were arguing in support of us. The Voluntary Euthanasia Society provided two affidavits.

The first was from the president of the VES, Jack Havill. He outlined his own experience as an intensive care doctor, and how his interactions with dying patients had crystallised his views on assisted dying. He had been involved in shutting off life support in hundreds of cases, nearly always with patient consent or with the consent of the family, and he said he failed to see the ethical distinction between this act and the act of prescribing or administering life-ending medication.

The other affidavit from the VES was by a Canadian historian, John Weaver, whose book *Sorrows of a Century* was about suicides in New Zealand between 1900 and 2000. After reviewing over 12,000 coronial inquests he found that between 5 and 8 per cent of suicides annually were committed by terminally or irremediably ill people. These findings provided strong support for the argument that, with assisted-dying legislation, at least some of those people might have lived longer.

The Care Alliance was limited to presenting affidavits on the effects of assisted dying on the disabled community. The first was presented by Wendi Wicks and Robyn Hunt, key members of Not Dead Yet Aotearoa. They outlined examples of public services discriminating against the disabled, and of societal attitudes causing the physically impaired psychological distress and making them vulnerable to abuse. The affidavit went on to assert that legalising assisted dying for the terminally ill would somehow compel the disabled to consider assisted dying as an option, and that doctors might promote or even recommend assisted suicide to someone with an advanced disability.

These concerns have not been borne out in any country that has implemented assisted dying. In every jurisdiction with assisted-dying laws, a patient must explicitly request assisted dying: doctors cannot bring it up as an option and if they do they risk being reviewed for professional misconduct. It doesn't matter if the patient is terminal, or disabled, or depressed. The rules are clear. A complaint from a patient is all it would take for a doctor to be investigated and potentially disciplined.

Lecretia and I both supported disability rights: Lecretia was fast becoming disabled herself, and had availed herself of the many concessions and public services that our society offers disabled people, but we could not see how those rights extended to entrenching the suffering of the terminally ill.

Dr Huhana Hickey, a founding member of Not Dead Yet Aotearoa, submitted an affidavit that was a personal account of how assisted-dying legislation would affect her. Dr Hickey has primary progressive multiple sclerosis. If Lecretia decided that her life was not worth living because of her symptoms, others might decide that Dr Hickey's life was not worth living, she argued, and that might influence her own self-view. This ignored the fact that not one of Lecretia's family members, or friends, or witnesses would ever assert that Lecretia's life was not worth living, and no one was making that point now. This would be her own assessment, made according to her own values. The judgments of others were irrelevant, carrying no weight, and nor would they carry any weight in Dr Hickey's case.

The one example that Dr Hickey cited was the 2012 case of the forty-five-year-old Belgian Verbessem twins, Marc and Eddy, who had been born deaf but were about to go blind, too, and who opted to be assisted to die. She called this 'chilling evidence that an idea that starts with compassion can readily lead directly to the killing of people with disabilities because of their disabilities'. But not only were the twins acting in accordance with their own wishes, which they made clear to their doctor and their family, but their deafness and imminent blindness were compounded by other degenerative health problems. It has since been revealed by Australian broadcaster Andrew Denton that the family of the twins are distressed that their case is used by anti-assisted-dying advocates as an example of Belgian laws gone wrong. It is hurtful to the twins' family, and disrespectful to the twins. According to the twins and their family, the decision was freely made, after months of discussion with the family doctor, and not undertaken lightly. It was well within the parameters set out by Belgian law.

The weekend after we received the interveners' affidavits, Geoffrey Palmer and his wife Margaret hosted a dinner for Lecretia in Wellington. Friends came from Auckland and from Christchurch. Lecretia was now in a wheelchair, unable to walk unassisted, and her appearance was possibly a shock to some. Her right eye squinted and her left bulged, giving her face an uneven appearance. Her left hand hung uselessly in her lap. Her speech was slurred. But these things were of no import to her, and she enjoyed herself immensely. She beamed as friends arrived, and was delighted to catch up with all the gossip. She took the chance to pin down her counsel, Andrew Butler, who was also there, and quiz him about the affidavits thus far.

Our plan the following week was for Lecretia and I to spend a few days in Auckland, eating and drinking and having fun. But sadly it was becoming apparent that travel was going to be almost impossible. Lecretia's sense of her own body was failing her—her need to go to the bathroom was often sudden and insistent, but being in a wheelchair, her ability to get there was diminished. Negotiating taxis and flights and unfamiliar hotel lobbies and restaurants all seemed too difficult, and I cancelled the trip. Lecretia was upset, and I told her I would make it up to her.

The defendants' affidavits arrived after 9 May, and I began the task of reading them to Lecretia, as the words swam when she tried.

Many of the affidavits made her angry. The most irritating, arguing on behalf of the attorney-general, was that of Baroness Ilora Finlay, a professor of palliative medicine active in the anti-assisted-dying movement. She had visited New Zealand in 2012, funded by the Catholic Church, and had spoken about palliative care.

Although Ilora Finlay admitted in her affidavit that palliative care is not a panacea, she stated that advances in palliative care had lessened the need for assisted dying.

She implied that in cases of patients seeking assistance to die, something else was at work beneath the surface: vulnerability, coercion, a lack of mental capacity, a doctor's influence. None of these things applied to Lecretia. The baroness claimed there had been an increase in suicides in Oregon and the Netherlands after assisted dying had become legal. She took issue with Dr Munglani's evidence on pain management, Dr Smales' real-world experience and Dr Ashby's statements on the value of holistic care. She did not refer to Lecretia much, but claimed that the way to add quality to someone's life was to listen. But the implication, as I saw it, was that one should listen without hearing, ignoring the patient's clear and consistent requests. The baroness recommended distracting the patient—perhaps, incredibly, by providing a hairdresser. She thought that reducing Lecretia's steroids might improve her mood and attitude. We had tried getting Lecretia off steroids multiple times, at Lecretia's request, but all that happened was that she suffered blinding headaches.

Reading the affidavit, I got the sense of someone who was well-meaning and kind-hearted, but who fundamentally saw her views and her perspective as superior to those of the patient. Her philosophy was diametrically opposed to Lecretia's. If all that palliative care could offer was a wholesale rejection of Lecretia's personal values of freedom, choice and the primacy of the patient's beliefs over the doctor's, then it was failing us, and failing others.

Etienne Montero, professor of law at the University of Namur in Belgium, discussed the impact of legislation in Belgium, explaining the controls and safeguards, and its potential expansion to include minors and the mentally unwell. Like Dr Hickey, he cited the case of the Verbessem twins as troublesome. One got the impression he was morally opposed to the choices people were making under Belgian law. It's worth noting that Montero's evidence was dismissed in *Carter v Canada*, the judge saying:

> We are not convinced that Professor Montero's evidence undermines the trial judge's findings of fact. First, the trial judge (rightly, in our view) noted that the permissive regime in Belgium is the product of a very different medico-legal culture. Practices of assisted death were 'already prevalent and embedded in the medical culture' prior to legalization. The regime simply regulates a common pre-existing practice. In the absence of a comparable history in Canada, the trial judge concluded that it was problematic to draw inferences about the level of physician compliance with legislated safeguards based on the Belgian evidence. This distinction is relevant both in assessing the degree

of physician compliance and in considering evidence with regards to the potential for a slippery slope.

Second, the cases described by Professor Montero were the result of an oversight body exercising discretion in the interpretation of the safeguards and restrictions in the Belgian legislative regime—a discretion the Belgian parliament has not moved to restrict. These cases offer little insight into how a Canadian regime might operate.

Tony O'Brien, an Irish palliative care physician, also outlined the value of palliative care. He made a helpful distinction between the types of requests to die: those that were really a cry for help, and those that were genuine. Unlike Baroness Finlay, he acknowledged the latter group:

> This group (an important minority) express a clear and consistent wish to exercise the right to have their life ended at a time, in a place and in a manner of their choosing. Typically, these patients are not depressed and they do not ordinarily exhibit features of other mental illness. In contrast, they are commonly quite intelligent, controlling and analytic people who feel the need to continue to exercise the greatest possible level of control over their destiny.

He also acknowledged that palliative care had its limitations. O'Brien's view, however, was in line with the judge's in the case that Marie Fleming, who suffered from multiple sclerosis, brought to the Irish High Court in 2012.

> 'If this court could tailor-make a solution,' the judge said, 'which would suit the needs of Ms Fleming alone without any possible implications for third parties or society at large, there might be a good deal to be said for her case. But the court cannot be so satisfied.'

The Fleming case was problematic for us, as the circumstances were similar to Lecretia's, but the judge had found against her. O'Brien was right to bring it up. We would have to deal with it. That said, in Fleming's case the judge noted that there was nothing stopping the state crafting a law to allow assisted dying, as although Ireland may be constitutionally required by the right to life to discourage suicide generally, it may not be required to in cases like Ms Fleming's.

Simon Allan, director of palliative care at Arohanui Hospice in Palmerston North, discussed palliative care in some detail, acknowledging that, for a small number of patients, the only effective way to deal with their pain was terminal sedation, the very death Lecretia didn't want. Mr Allan did not, however, fear assisted-dying legislation. Instead, he acknowledged that, though a regime might cause a divide in the medical profession, for palliative carers, it would be 'business as usual', as palliative carers would neither be asked to prescribe life-ending medication, nor help with it being administered. That responsibility would fall to individual GPs.

Dr Harvey Chochinov, professor of psychiatry and director of the Manitoba Palliative Care Research Unit, described his research into the concept of patient dignity, acknowledging that it meant different things to different patients, and required different approaches from carers. He acknowledged that there will always be those who want the option of assisted dying, and that palliative care 'will never be the perfect foil to suffering'. He took issue with some of Justice Lynn Smith's statements in her judgment in *Carter v Canada*, and described scenarios in which starving or dehydration until death were 'normal', and how their negative effects could be palliated.

It was a strong submission.

After I finished reading it to her, Lecretia paused for thought. What she wanted was an outcome that reflected her autonomy and free will. Chochinov's arguments, and the idea of having a normal death, if that meant days of starving and dehydration, were of no comfort to her.

Dr Amanda Landers, palliative care physician and chair of the Australian and New Zealand Society of Palliative Medicine, outlined the policy and position of the ANZSPM. While acknowledging that assisted dying happens, she denied that 'bumping up' of pain medication was a form of euthanasia, as the intent is to relieve suffering, and not to hasten death. This is often called the 'double effect'. When medicine relieves pain but hastens the death of a dying patient, a doctor can take refuge in the idea that their only intent is to relieve pain. Lecretia and I held the view that this was in effect a conscious self-deception and that some doctors knew exactly what they were doing. True intent in these cases is almost impossible to determine, and suggesting that all doctors have the same intentions is not something that can be proven or demonstrated.

Dr Sinéad Donnelly from Wellington acknowledged that palliative care is imperfect, but believed that Lecretia would not be at risk of an undignified death. She rejected assisted dying and the sense of control and autonomy it might give patients, saying that palliative care had answers for that. But she did acknowledge death is different for everyone, an entirely individual experience. But what she would not accept is that all of those differences are worthy of the same respect.

Roderick Macleod, an Auckland palliative care physician, acknowledged that some pain can be difficult to manage, citing a World Health Organization paper, which suggested up to 10 per cent of patients experience pain that is difficult to control. Despite this, he outlined his opposition to assisted dying and its possible effects on the medical profession. Finally, Dr John Kleinsman provided his view of the ethics of assisted dying, as director of the Nathaniel Centre, a Catholic bioethics think tank. He called upon the Hippocratic oath. He argued that the issue of elder abuse (a real problem, worthy of serious attention) was a justification for barring assisted suicide. These sorts of assertions, like the potential abuse of the disabled, are disingenuous, and suggest that it is excusable to ignore the plight of the terminally ill, and that their suffering is justified, to keep others from being afraid.

When I'd finished reading the affidavits to her, I looked at Lecretia with some relief. We had expected to see some worrying evidence that we hadn't yet encountered, or some argument we hadn't considered. But it was largely the same evidence that had been presented in *Carter v Canada*, a case that had been won. It gave us hope.

'What was the name of that doctor?' she said. 'The one from Manitoba?'

'Chochinov?'

'Yes. The sound of his name reminded me to ask you something.'

'What's that?'

'Is there any chocolate in the house?'

Chapter 20

LECRETIA'S *SUNDAY* STORY was due to be aired on 17 May. On the day of the broadcast, Lecretia's family came to Wellington, and we went out to Logan Brown, a local restaurant, for lunch. Lecretia was now too tired in the evenings to go out to dinner. When we left the house, she now needed to be moved around in a wheelchair. My father had been down to visit and had built wooden ramps to be laid over the steps into our home, so that she could be taken from the living room up to the road without leaving her chair.

We discussed what we were expecting from the *Sunday* episode. For me, the worst possible outcome would have been a tear-jerker story which didn't push the issue forward. In my short experience of public life, I had learned that no matter what you want the story to be, others will decide it for you. All you can do is to be your authentic self, and hope that the truth of the story will come through unscathed. Lecretia hoped the same, but was also anxious about how she might appear on camera. She didn't like the idea of being on television, but she believed that any embarrassment she felt would be worth it if it made an impact.

I had also been asked if I would be willing to go on breakfast television the day after *Sunday* aired, as they planned to play Lecretia's challenge to the prime minister to change the law, and they wanted to give me the opportunity to respond to his on-camera comments. Lecretia was not well enough to appear herself, and the responsibility had fallen to me. It wasn't something I'd anticipated and I was reluctant to do it, nervous about how it might interfere with my professional life. Would Xero be upset about me speaking out on such a contentious issue? What would happen in meetings with clients and partners if people knew I was an assisted-dying advocate?

On the Sunday night, we settled down to watch the program. *Sunday*'s ratings were typically between 400,000 and 600,000 viewers, so between 9 and 13 per cent of New Zealand's population would be tuned in. Lecretia sat in her electric armchair with the footrest raised, a blanket over her and Ferdinand perched between her legs on the footrest. She was in good spirits, but apprehensive about the screening.

The story itself was impressive. It addressed Lecretia's legal challenge, but it was a human story too: it was hard not to be moved by Lecretia's quiet determination. Her tone was measured, positive and clear: she came across as utterly reasonable, which of course she was. When it was over, my phone and Lecretia's immediately began beeping. People started visiting Lecretia's Facebook page, wanting to know more about her, and she started getting a huge number of social media followers. In the space of less than an hour, Lecretia Seales was a household name.

I suddenly felt very protective of her. Would she be strong enough to deal with all this attention? The High Court hearing, at which all the written evidence would be heard and discussed, was due to begin on Monday 25 May, just over a week away. But she was very determined to appear in court. It wasn't long before she was asking me to re-read many of the affidavits that we'd already reviewed, so that she could reflect on the arguments before they were heard in court.

On Monday, I drove down to the TVNZ studio in Wellington. I'd never been on TV before, and I was being asked to respond to the prime minister, who was in the studio in Auckland, live on air. I was mic'ed up and faced the barrel of the camera.

The program started with a clip from the *Sunday* program in which Lecretia directly addressed the prime minister and challenged him to change the law. John Key responded by declaring his position—that it was a matter of conscience, implying that it should be dealt with as a private member's bill. Personally he supported assisted dying, he said, adding that he would probably vote for assisted-dying legislation if it came before the house and was reasonably circumscribed; he also said he had a lot of sympathy and respect for Lecretia. This was a victory. A week earlier, questions about assisted dying would have been deftly avoided by most politicians, but now our country's leader was discussing his views openly on television. After months of silence, assisted dying was a public issue again.

I got the chance to respond, and acknowledged and built on John Key's statements, agreeing that it was a conscience issue, but suggesting possible ways that the government could take it forward other than a private member's bill—by putting a government bill on the order paper and putting it up for a conscience vote, or conducting a parliamentary inquiry, or referring the matter to the

Law Commission. Though the prime minister did not get a chance to respond to my suggestions, this was a good result. At this point it was enough to have him talking about the issue—parliament was not in a position to do anything until the High Court case was resolved. Raising awareness was the best we could hope for, so that once the hearing concluded there would be enough public interest for parliament to take action, whatever the outcome. At the end of the interview the cameraman removed my mic. My hands were clammy, and shaking. I left the building and drove home.

Shirley and Larry were still staying with us. They had seen the interview and were impressed. Rod Drury, my boss's boss at Xero, had texted to congratulate me. I felt pretty good. Lecretia was oblivious, fast asleep in bed. She wasn't getting up much earlier than 10 am by then, so the 7 am broadcast was way too early for her. When she did get up a bit later, she was interested, but more interested in being wheeled out to the dining room table, where she could eat her favourite breakfast: homemade muesli, plain yoghurt and blueberries. While she ate I dispensed her various medications, which we had now augmented with metformin and atorvastatin, drugs that were not typically prescribed but for which there was mounting evidence of efficacy against cancer, along with the herbal stuff: turmeric and Salvestrol. The pills were a meal in themselves, there were so many of them. But Lecretia swallowed each without complaint, washing away their bitter taste with mouthfuls of muesli.

In the following days, Lecretia and her lawyers worked on our reply affidavits, which gave us a chance to provide additional information and respond to the Crown's evidence. These were collated as written testimonies, like the previous affidavits, and once submitted they would complete all the written materials necessary for the hearing.

Lecretia's affidavits were the first to be sworn. She was interviewed by Catherine Marks while she reclined in her chair, and asked for her response to the evidence that had been written by the Crown's witnesses. Her first affidavit was a reply to Baroness Finlay's, asserting that the baroness's concerns about coercion, vulnerability and depression did not apply in Lecretia's case. Lecretia concluded by saying:

> Baroness Finlay discusses the need to listen carefully and sensitively to terminal patients' needs in order to improve their sense of wellbeing. That is exactly what I am asking for in my case. I would like my wish not to have to suffer unnecessarily at the end of my life to be respected, rather than to be told that my own choices are unsafe or cannot be trusted.

In her second affidavit, she responded to the other crown witnesses. She complimented the work of palliative carers and expressed gratitude for the care she'd received so far, but then outlined her concerns: the need for strangers to visit her house, or shower her, which she didn't like. She discussed her symptoms and how palliative care drugs did not help her with them, and how the changes she was undergoing caused her psychological distress. The unwinding skein of her life was blowing free in the wind, and it tormented her. She wanted to control her destiny. The freedom to take life-ending medication if she wished would give her that.

She objected to the evidence of Dr Chochinov, denying that she felt hopeless or lacked self-worth. She vehemently objected to the views of Robert George, who had said that expert palliative care allowed a dying person to 'explore other perspectives and realities', thereby transcending their current suffering:

> This does not resonate with me or the person I am in any respect. Indeed, it is almost insulting to me to suggest my very considered views and assessment of my situation are somehow unreliable and could be recast so that my suffering is imbued with meaning.

She rejected the idea of terminal sedation as an acceptable way to die that was consistent with who she was. She identified herself as part of a small group of people who have expressed a clear and consistent wish to die and are not masking some sort of untreated physical or psychological suffering. She argued that suffering is inherently unique to individuals and some suffering simply cannot be addressed through palliation. For Lecretia, freedom to choose when and how she died was the only thing that would address that suffering. Being forced to undergo unnecessary suffering would be intolerable to her.

She couldn't have been clearer.

The next affidavit was from Dr Linda Ganzini, who had conducted research into whether assisted-dying legislation in Oregon had affected vulnerable groups, such as the elderly, women, people without health insurance, people with AIDS, people with low educational status, the poor, racial and ethnic minorities, people with disabilities, minors and those with psychiatric illnesses. Her study found that none of these people were over-represented in any Oregon statistics, except those with AIDS, and that may have been due to the unavailability of effective AIDS drugs at the time of the study. Opponents have challenged Ganzini's study many times, but their objections always come up short as the data is thoroughly clear. The findings were upheld in *Carter v Canada*, the case that brought assisted-dying laws to Canada. The Oregon laws were working. No one has been able to produce a peer-reviewed study which contradicts Ganzini's findings.

Dr Ganzini also took issue with some of the figures Baroness Finlay had quoted. The baroness had asserted that in Oregon assisted dying was primarily used by people older than sixty-five. Dr Ganzini was able to show that it was more common in younger terminally ill patients, where the patient's youth might cause them to take a long time to die. She also showed that Baroness Finlay's statistics overstated the number of patients receiving treatment for clinical depression who had received help to die—it was 16.7 per cent, closer to one in six than one in three.

She also demonstrated that statistics can be presented to sound more alarming than they actually are. For example, Baroness Finlay had said the number of patients who received help to die in Oregon each year had increased by six and a half times since the act was passed, which sounds frightening. But in raw terms, the numbers did not seem so dramatic: in the first year, twenty-four people had received prescriptions, increasing to 155 in 2014, with only 105 ultimately taking the medication. This represented only 0.31 per cent of all deaths in Oregon in 2014.

Baroness Finlay pointed out that 40 per cent of patients cited being a burden as the reason for seeking assisted dying, a proportion which might seem to indicate coercion, but

Dr Ganzini noted that under Oregon law a patient can nominate multiple reasons. The other significant reasons chosen by patients were losing autonomy (91 per cent), inability to engage in activities, making life less enjoyable (87 per cent), loss of dignity (71 per cent) and losing control of bodily functions (50 per cent). Being a burden was way down the list, and was in itself no evidence of coercion.

The affidavit of Professor Udo Schuklenk, a bioethicist, outlined the findings of a Royal Society of Canada inquiry into end-of-life decision-making, conducted by a panel of five bioethicists and health professionals which he had chaired. Dr Schuklenk had made it clear from the outset that he would not support decriminalisation unless he could be completely satisfied that 'slippery slope' arguments were not warranted. The panel reviewed evidence from Belgium, Luxembourg and the Netherlands, along with the four US states that had decriminalised assisted dying.

The panel concluded that evidence from other jurisdictions did not support the causal slippery slope argument, and noted: 'The factors that proponents of this argument identify point towards safeguards that could be implemented, rather than towards total prohibition.' It also found that prohibition would not prevent lives lost through assisted death, because assisted dying happens anyway. Its argument was that the practice would continue even if it remained prohibited, and that there were moral costs associated with prohibition, including 'needless suffering and thwarting of autonomy'.

Although the panel strongly endorsed efforts to improve the quality of palliative care, it concluded that not all patients want palliative care, and nor can palliative care help all patients. In addition, it asserted that society should not have to wait until palliative care reaches perfection before it recognises a terminally ill person's right to be assisted to die at a time of their choosing.

In short, the panel's findings were the same as Justice Lynn Smith's. In summary, Dr Schuklenk said:

> We tested the evidence as academics. Justice Lynn Smith saw it tested under courtroom conditions (and her views were upheld by the Supreme Court of Canada). Quebec has tested the evidence under legislative conditions. I take comfort from the fact that we have all come to the same conclusions.

Dr Schuklenk also reviewed the affidavits of the witnesses for the Crown. He said that their claims of coercion and vulnerability were unsubstantiated by evidence, and that the absolute ethical principles asserted by some of them were not universally held. Many secular ethicists believe that the only question that matters from the patient's perspective is whether death is in the patient's best interest. The method by which that is achieved, given the patient's voluntary, competent request, is moot, whether via withdrawal of treatment, taking of life-ending medication, or being administered a drug by the doctor.

Baroness Finlay had implied that suicides in Oregon had increased since the passage of its Death with Dignity Act and were above the national average. Dr Schuklenk was able to show that the suicide rate in Oregon has always been above the national average, and that the introduction of legislation did not see an increase in the trend at all. There was a decrease in the 1990s which reversed around 2000, but this pattern was seen throughout the United States. In the Netherlands, contrary to Baroness Finlay's claims, the suicide rate was no higher than the United Kingdom's. In 2012, the suicide rate in the UK was 11.6 suicides in every 100,000 deaths, compared with 10.6 in the Netherlands, and in fact the suicide rate in the Netherlands had gone down 4 per cent between 1995 and 2010. There was no evidence of any sort of suicide contagion—the idea that otherwise well patients would commit suicide at increased rates simply because the laws allowed terminally ill patients to be assisted to die.

Addressing the increase in the number of assisted deaths in Oregon, from 0.09 per cent of deaths to 0.31 per cent of deaths, he said: 'It is not surprising that a new service provided by a health care system would experience an increasing number of users over time. The increase in numbers does not constitute evidence of an abusive system.' He acknowledged that a small number of Oregon patients reported depression (three out of eighteen patients in the study cited, or 16.7 per cent), but noted that depressive patients are not necessarily unable to make competent choices. Then, in response to the argument that safeguards would never be safe enough, he stated that although no system is ever 100 per cent effective, the risk of abuse can be thoroughly minimised and needs to be assessed against the benefits to patients. He also said, 'When the outcome is the same—death—why in one case are safeguards that are less than 100 per cent effective not acceptable (assisted dying) but in the second case acceptable (withdrawing medical treatments)?'

Regarding Dr Kleinsman's references to the Hippocratic oath, he said, 'This oath has limited value in the modern world. I note for example that it also prohibits doctors from practising surgery ... As of 2002, only one of the twelve medical schools in Australia and New Zealand was using a modified version of the Hippocratic oath in its graduation ceremonies.'

Richard Owens, professor of psychology at Auckland University, responded to the affidavits of Amanda Landers and Sinéad Donnelly and introduced in his new affidavit a survey he had conducted revealing that doctors in New Zealand essentially admitted that they were hastening death without request, and at the same rates as doctors in the Netherlands were hastening death without request before assisted-dying legislation was introduced, and that the availability of palliative care had no effect on physicians' decisions to do so. It also revealed that, alarmingly, in over half the New Zealand cases there was no discussion with the patient beforehand, despite almost a quarter of those patients being judged as competent. These cases, in which doctors ended their patients' lives without an explicit request from the patient, accounted for 2.7 per cent of all deaths in New Zealand. Deaths of this type are much less frequent in the Netherlands and Belgium since assisted-dying legislation was enacted.

Professor Owens also argued that it was naive to quote the maxim 'first do no harm' as a defence against assisted dying, and gave the example of cutting off someone's legs: it does harm, but may be the best option in some circumstances.

In response to Roderick Macleod's statement that pain can be relieved in 90 per cent of patients, he argued that this fact was no comfort to the 'small but significant' group of people whom, by implication, doctors are unable to treat adequately. Owens finished by noting: 'The slow improvement of palliative care possible over the longer term is of no benefit to those who cannot be helped *right now*.'

Colin Gavaghan, associate professor of law at Otago University in New Zealand, gave his views on the bioethics of assisted dying, and the positions held by New Zealand medical bodies. He asserted that there was no ethical distinction between helping a patient to die and withdrawing life-preserving treatment. In both cases, the physician knows that death will be the outcome. He also pointed out that a doctor may prescribe a life-ending drug to a patient without knowing whether they will actually take it, whereas a doctor withdrawing life-sustaining ventilation or hydration knows exactly what the outcome will be.

He quoted from *Principles of Biomedical Ethics* by Tom L. Beauchamp and James F. Childress:

> Correctly labelling an act as 'killing' or as 'letting die', therefore, does not determine that one form of action is better or worse, or more or less justified, than the other. Some particular instance of killing (a brutal murder, say) may be worse than some particular instance of allowing someone to die (e.g., forgoing treatment for a patient who is in a persistent vegetative state); but some particular instance of

letting die (not resuscitating a patient who could be saved, say) also may be worse than some particular instance of killing (such as mercy killing at the patient's request) ... We may need to know about the actor's motive (whether it is benevolent or malicious, for example), the patient's or surrogate's request, or the act's consequences. These additional factors will allow us to place the act on a moral map and make a normative judgment about it.

This was the essence of the debate for me. The rules were inflexible, unable to accommodate complex situations in which a sophisticated moral judgment was called for. The laws were tipped too far towards outright prohibition, leading medicine to do the *wrong* thing, while doctors wanting to abide by their patients' wishes could only do so by flouting the law.

As for autonomy, Associate Professor Gavaghan said:

I am unaware of any credible account of autonomy that asserts it 'essentially knows no limits'. Even John Stuart Mill, widely hailed as the foremost champion of personal liberty, recognised that this could legitimately be restrained to prevent harm to others. But a serious commitment to respect for autonomy requires more than merely speculative or remote threats of such harm. Rather, the onus rests with those who would restrict autonomy to demonstrate a compelling need to do so.

Dr Libby Smales, Dr Rajesh Munglani and Dr Michael Ashby introduced affidavits clarifying earlier statements in response to some of the criticisms Baroness Finlay had offered. Dr Ashby noted that the claims made in several of the defendants' affidavits were irrelevant to the case, as they did not apply to Lecretia. She was not incompetent, vulnerable, unaware of her options, or depressed, and she had not been coerced, so it was simply incorrect to assert that her request was irrational on the basis of any of those factors.

Regarding the assertion that it was impossible to design a system in which every medical procedure will be completed perfectly, free of error, Dr Ashby gave the example of open-heart surgery, a commonly used medical procedure. It is not banned even though errors occasionally occur in the operating theatre. There are always risks, but as long as patients are aware of those risks, they can elect to undergo a procedure or not.

He agreed that palliative care had made significant advances, but said the idea that Lecretia should wait until it had attained some hypothetical state of perfection, a target that might never be reached, was ridiculous. I agreed. To my mind, it was as ridiculous as asking Lecretia to wait for a cure for brain cancer. In her terminal state, she did not have the time to wait for either of these solutions.

Tony O'Brien had given the examples of Stephen Hawking and Jean-Dominique Bauby as evidence that dependence and impaired mobility are not incompatible with quality of life. Dr Ashby simply observed that Professor Hawking had publicly supported the UK's assisted-dying bill, and discussed some of the thresholds at which he would like to have the choice to be assisted to die.

Dr Munglani was questioned by Baroness Finlay about his claim that he'd very frequently seen cases of excruciating pain unresponsive to analgesics, requiring heavy sedation. She had questioned him about this once before, in 2014, when there was an assisted-dying debate before the House of Lords in Britain. At the time, she emailed him and said this did not accord with her experience and asked for evidence. He provided a wealth of supporting evidence to the baroness in an eighteen-page email, which included the views of his colleagues, who generally supported his position, and numerous citations from studies supporting his claims. Dr Munglani included this email as an exhibit in Lecretia's case, and noted that the baroness had not responded to any of that evidence in her affidavit.

Dr Eric Kress, a medical director at the Hospice of Missoula, Montana, explored how Montana had changed since a court ruling in 2009 which found that doctors in that state would not be subject to prosecution if they helped patients to die. In short, he said that it hadn't changed much at all. Patients weren't worried about pressure from doctors, and there was no drop in hospice enrolments. For those who were concerned about controlling their circumstances, however, the possibility of an assisted death gave them much relief.

He confirmed that there was no compulsion for doctors to participate. Upon being asked for assistance, Dr Kress would review the patient's files, consult specialists, attempt to understand the patient's motivations, and ensure that no underlying factor, such as poorly controlled pain, had contributed to the request. He was surprised at Baroness Finlay's assertion that doctors would 'view the death of a patient as a solution to the problem they present'. He did not feel that way at all: his primary motivation was to ameliorate suffering. He regarded aid in dying as a last resort. In the six years since the law had been clarified, he said he had written ten prescriptions for patients who had asked him to help them die. 'All of those patients were of sound mind, none was depressed and not one of them was suicidal,' he said. 'They all loved life and told me they would prefer to live, but not in the miserable conditions the disease had imposed on them.'

He went on to discuss other methods patients can use to exercise some control over the manner of their deaths, including palliative sedation and refusing life-prolonging interventions. He noted that these options are not considered to be suicide, even when the patient clearly chooses them in order to hasten death. He said he agreed with that position, and also considered that aid in dying is not suicide.

He explained:

I frequently know the families of my patients and I have seen that family members of a patient who chooses aid in dying are glad that their loved one was able to achieve a peaceful death, at home, surrounded by loved ones. This was certainly true for the three patients that asked me to be present when they took the medication. The family members of patients that have chosen aid in dying have universally been grateful to me for allowing the patient to have a peaceful death. I am familiar with a study that shows that none of the adverse impacts known to afflict survivors of someone who has committed suicide are experienced by survivors of patients who choose aid in dying. My experience is consistent with the findings in that study.

Philip Patston, a New Zealand disability campaigner, replied to the affidavits presented by Dr Hickey, Wendi Wicks and Robyn Hunt on behalf of the Care Alliance. Patston, who uses a wheelchair and lives with cerebral palsy, said in his affidavit:

> I find their arguments patronising. They amount to saying that members of the disabled community have such a low sense of self-worth that the availability of assisted dying would make them feel obliged to end their lives in order to avoid being a burden on others. In my opinion there is no justification for projecting that view onto an entire category of society. I doubt the witnesses for the Care Alliance have such a low sense of self-worth. I certainly do not.

He felt that disabled people were more at risk from suicide-related harm under the current laws than they would be if assisted dying were legal, and that conflating the issues of disability discrimination and assisted dying was not useful for disabled people, or for people suffering a terminal illness. He said that as a disabled person, he valued his right to live, and he wanted the right to choose to end his life in the case of acute suffering. In his conversations with other members of the disabled community, he found broad support for these views. It was clear from Mr Patston's affidavit that the Care Alliance and Not Dead Yet

Aotearoa did not speak for the entire disabled community, and possibly only for a very small part of it.

Dr Grube and Dr Reagan, of Oregon, addressed concerns about the potential impact of assisted dying voiced by some of the witnesses for the defence. They worried that assisted dying might harm the doctor–patient relationship, or the quality and availability of palliative care. Dr Grube pointed out that none of that had happened in Oregon. A majority of doctors in Oregon now supported assisted dying, even though some don't participate. No doctor is compelled to do so, and others work at institutions that don't allow it.

He added: 'I reject any suggestion that legalisation of assisted dying leads doctors to lose sight of treating the distress of their patients, and to focus instead on providing aid in dying. Compassionate doctors, in my opinion, pay attention to their patients' needs, symptoms, disease, and so on. They honour their patients' autonomy, ensure the patient is giving informed consent, spend hours explaining the patients' issues, and ultimately do not restrict legal options from their patients. They care.

'In the USA, if you listen to the tone of many of those (including doctors) who are opposed to aid in dying, you find a surprising amount of anger and irritability, scolding, and guilt and shame-flavoured statements. In my view it is they who have lost sight of treating the distress of their patient, and who prevent their patient from a dignified death.'

He also observed that palliative care in Oregon had expanded after the Death with Dignity Act was passed. Ninety-three per cent of patients who consider assisted dying are in hospice care. He said that the patients he treated and who obtained prescriptions under the Death with Dignity Act were not suicidal or mentally ill, and were not acting impulsively or alone, but within a community, with their family, their hospice, and their physician.

Dr Reagan expressed the view that the doctor–patient relationship had changed, but in a positive way. A request for aid in dying dramatically deepened the relationship between the doctor and their patient, and the patient's family, too. He said that he found these cases tough and emotionally draining, even after more than fifteen years working in this area, but he thought that was as it should be: it should not be an easy option, it should be a last resort.

He noted that obtaining a prescription is a big commitment, and it takes a lot of effort on the patient's part, because doctors want to avoid it if they can, but those patients who go through with it feel much more at ease afterwards, and experience far less distress.

I read all these and other affidavits to Lecretia as she

reclined in her electric armchair, eating feijoas. It took days to get through all the material, and I frequently had to drink water to keep my throat from getting parched. I'd never talked so much in my life. When it was done, she was pleased: she felt the Crown's case was weak and was looking forward to getting into the courtroom.

Lecretia's lawyers also prepared a submission, a long document that outlined their interpretation of the Bill of Rights Act and the Crimes Act, drawing heavily on the evidence that had been submitted by both their witnesses and the Crown. It outlined how dignity is a key aspect of the right to life, and that this principle had been upheld in previous court decisions. The submission laid out a case for not prosecuting Lecretia's doctor—the best result we could hope for—or at least declaring an infringement of Lecretia's rights.

Though Lecretia was interested in the case, she had a more pressing concern. She'd organised for the commissioners from the Law Commission to visit her at home, to discuss the status of her last project with the commission: a review of the laws of contempt of court. On the Tuesday before the case, the four commissioners and the general manager crowded into our small lounge, bringing with them almond croissants from Louis Sergeant's that Lecretia had demanded as the price of admission.

The commissioners brought Lecretia up to speed, but it was becoming clear that, in Lecretia's short absence from the office, her work had moved beyond her. She had trouble following the thread of the conversation and appeared to lose interest. But the visit was symbolic: an acknowledgment of her contribution to the Law Commission. Simply by visiting Lecretia the commissioners paid her tribute. She sat in her armchair in the corner of the room, legs raised, one eye swollen shut and her head nodding, while the commissioners spoke about how the work would continue, incorporating her contributions.

Before the commissioners left, I asked them for a photograph with Lecretia, and they obliged. Five venerable gentlemen at the pinnacle of their legal careers, and Lecretia in the foreground in her wheelchair, a rug over her legs, looking slightly diminished. And yet she was the focus of the image, the subject that drew the eye.

Later that afternoon I spoke to Lecretia and asked her what she wanted to do. Officially she was still on unpaid leave from the commission. She had held on to the job because her intent was to get better and return to her nineteenth-floor office with its beautiful views of the harbour. But something had changed, and when I suggested that she might think about resigning, she gave her consent.

I called the general manager, a quiet and kind man named Roland Daysh. I thanked him for organising the commissioners' visit, and informed him that Lecretia would like to resign. He accepted the resignation with some relief. The commission had been kind in keeping Lecretia's role open, knowing that her work was such an important part of her identity, but had already sensed that she would not return. Tuesday 19 May 2015, six days before the *Seales v Attorney-General* hearing, was the last day of Lecretia's seven-year career with the Law Commission.

Despite her declining health, Lecretia's blood counts had improved, so her oncologist was willing to let her try temozolomide again. It was her last hope, but recalling the dramatically positive effect it had after our trip to Argentina, we felt it was worth a go.

I was still feeling guilty about cancelling our trip to Auckland, so I organised for a local chef, a young man named Sam Pope, to come and cook for Lecretia. We worked on the menu together: him presenting ideas and me choosing dishes that I thought would appeal to my wife. We chose five courses: Jerusalem artichoke and porcini soup, seared salmon with remoulade, confit duck leg with lentils and a plum relish, slow-cooked lamb with fondant potatoes and beans, and rich chocolate dessert to finish. I wanted to surprise her. I invited her closest friend, Angela, and Angela's husband, Ben, and Shirley, too.

Sam arrived and greeted me at the door. He'd spent the day preparing his ingredients, and brought a restaurant's worth of supplies and equipment into our kitchen, requiring only the use of our stove to cook and assemble our meal. At the right moment I wheeled Lecretia up to the dining room table, which I'd laid out with printed menus and place settings. She was delighted.

Sam had cut up Lecretia's dishes so that she could negotiate them with the fork in her right hand. I would turn her plate in the middle of each course, so that the left-hand side, which her brain ignored, became the right. She lingered over the food, savouring every mouthful. It was a far sight better than the dishes I had served up over the last couple of weeks. When the dessert arrived, she took the tiniest morsels with every spoonful, as though wanting it to last forever.

When the evening was at an end, I wheeled Lecretia into the bedroom and helped her out of the wheelchair. I sat her on the bed, and helped her undress and get into our bed. She fell asleep almost immediately, a half-smile on her face.

The next day we received the Crown's submissions for the first time, laying out their case. It was narrowly focused on the interpretation of the law. But that made sense, in a way. If the Crown started debating the ethics of assisted dying, the case moved from an argument about whether it was legally possible to whether it was morally permissible, so instead the emphasis was on the intent of the relevant provisions of the Crimes Act. But Lecretia was ready. It was time to fight for her life, and control of her death.

Chapter 21

ON MONDAY 25 MAY, the first day of the hearing, I woke up next to Lecretia while she still dozed beside me. I got up and went to talk to her mother. We'd decided on a division of responsibilities: Larry and I would head to the court, while she and Jeremy would bring Lecretia to the court later.

Despite Lecretia's determination to be at the court-room, her body was not cooperating. She now slept twelve hours every day. Even a week earlier she would have been upset to have been a minute late, but she was now indifferent about keeping time.

As we entered the court, I experienced my first media scrum. There were two tiers of photographers, some squatting, some standing, and the black lenses of their cameras were clustered together like the eyes of a spider. As Larry and I approached, their shutters clicked rapidly and hurried voices asked for comment.

We'd decided not to say anything. We didn't want to appear to be trying to influence the outcome of the case one way or another. All requests were answered in the same way. 'We're not speaking to the media out of respect for the judicial process.'

In the courtroom the judge's seat was behind a large bench on an elevated platform. In front of him sat the clerk, and then at floor level were the various counsel. Lecretia's team were at the very front of the courtroom; behind them sat the Crown, and the Human Rights Commission, and behind them the Care Alliance and the Voluntary Euthanasia Society. On the left side, facing the judge, were desks for media and the various reporters from the newspapers, radio and television. On the right side was the jury box, where Lecretia's friends and family were invited to sit. There was a desk for me, off to the side of that, where I could take notes. And beside me were a couple of video cameras, pointed away from me and the jury box, so that Lecretia and her family wouldn't be filmed. Lecretia's illness was becoming more pronounced, distorting her features. We wanted people to remember her as the person she was, not diminished by her illness.

The jury box began filling up with Lecretia's friends and family. One of Lecretia's aunts, Soraya, had come down from Auckland to follow the trial. Angela and Ben were there, along with Sonya, who had once told me I knew how to make Lecretia laugh. Jo Hughson, a barrister, was there too, and Sir Geoffrey Palmer. Geoffrey's son, Matthew Palmer, was also in the court, acting as counsel for the Human Rights Commission.

The public gallery was full. I recognised a few of the faces, which included Andrew Geddis, a law professor from Otago University, and several of Lecretia's colleagues from the Law Commission. There were also a few faces I knew from the media.

I laid eyes on the solicitor-general for the first time that day. Mike Heron was a youngish, handsome man who seemed to have slightly more panache than his assistant counsel Paul Rishworth. He came over and introduced himself to us. He was the opposition, but he was genuinely likeable, even if he did congratulate us for getting things 'this far'. Perhaps the subtle slight was a lawyer's tactic.

Finally, the hour arrived, and we were invited to rise by the court's clerk. Justice Collins made his entrance and invited us all to sit. He asked after Lecretia, and Andrew

Butler explained that she had not yet made it to the courtroom, but when she arrived perhaps the court could adjourn and allow her to enter. Justice Collins agreed.

Andrew's first remarks were about Lecretia herself. He reminded the judge that the case was about her circumstances, and he gave a long outline of her life and illness, and her motivations for wanting to have her claim heard by the High Court. He emphasised that Lecretia's medical witnesses had described the possibility of a painful death, and that vulnerability, coercion and incompetence were not factors in this case. All of the defence's evidence that suggested otherwise could be dismissed. While he laid out his case, occasionally coughing to clear his throat, the four other lawyers from Russell McVeagh passed him papers, shared their notes and took notes of their own.

I was impressed by Lecretia's lawyers. Along their expansive desk, facing the judge, they had arranged all of their papers in large binders, indexed and arrayed like books on a bookshelf. They looked like magicians in their robes, conjuring up truth as they made their arguments, shuffling papers and facts. This was the way legal decisions had been made for centuries. Only the traditional wigs were absent, a very modern omission.

Midmorning Lecretia and Shirley arrived. The court had given Lecretia a parking space in the basement, so she was able to enter the jury room unmolested by the media waiting out the front of the building. The information was relayed to Andrew. At the conclusion of his statements, he informed the judge.

The decision to adjourn was made, and I went to the jury room, where Lecretia was sitting in her wheelchair, sipping a cup of tea and nibbling on a chocolate brownie.

'Hello,' she said, smiling.

I told her how the case had begun, and then Andrew Butler came in and gave his interpretation of events. The boxy little room, absent of windows, with a large formica table in the middle and a whiteboard at the end, took on the aspect of a canteen, as people made coffee and chatted. After ten minutes or so, we made our way back into the courtroom. Someone held the door open as I wheeled Lecretia in, and all eyes were on her as she entered the room.

Lecretia sat with her feet out in front of her and her head leaned back. She could no longer bend at the waist very easily, and her left leg, very stiff, stuck out as though in a cast. Her left arm and hand were curled up against her stomach. Her hair, thin and matted, was curly against her skull. Her right eye was swollen shut, but her left eye gleamed. She was smiling, clearly pleased to see the results of her efforts. Despite her illness, she had an air of dignity. Her presence was powerful. This was not a hypothetical case. This was about a real person, and her real circumstances.

When Justice Collins returned, the court rose. Lecretia tried to rise out of her chair. Her mother and I gently dissuaded her, assuring her that it wasn't necessary. When Justice Collins invited the room to be seated, his first comments were to Lecretia, acknowledging her arrival and thanking her for being in court.

Lecretia listened as Andrew Butler continued to lay out his case. As the first part of the claim related to the legal definition of suicide, he discussed the differences between suicide and making a rational decision to die. He asked whether Lecretia, and people in similar circumstances, should be forced to die in ways that were inconsistent with their beliefs in order to uphold an assumption about the meaning of the law—would their human rights be infringed for the benefit of others?

Section 179 of the New Zealand Crimes Act makes it illegal to aid and abet suicide. But what if such a death wasn't suicide? And what was the purpose of this section anyway, if not to protect the vulnerable? Lecretia, as she had asserted in her affidavits, was not vulnerable, so wasn't it unfair that the law should prohibit her, and others like her, from seeking help to die, when they had made a rational decision to do so?

Next Andrew Butler discussed section 41 of the Crimes Act, which permits the use of reasonable force to prevent a suicide. Could someone assault a doctor who was attempting to remove treatment from a patient in a hospital, if that patient had asked for the doctor to do so? Does the law support the force-feeding of a patient who has chosen to starve to death—in effect a slow suicide? On certain readings of the law, it would appear that it did.

After Andrew spoke, his colleague Chris Curran began discussing the bill of rights, and how it applied to Lecretia. The Bill of Rights Act guarantees the right not to be deprived of life and not to be subjected to cruel and degrading treatment. But did the right to life mean that an individual was obliged to live at all costs, even if they felt their life had no quality? Did our laws, ostensibly secular, enshrine the religious principle of the sanctity of life?

During this discussion, Matthew Palmer was asked, as the representative of the Human Rights Commission, for his views on the bill of rights and how it applied to Lecretia's case. He assured Justice Collins that if he found a breach of rights, the means were there for him to make a declaration. A declaration of this type had never been made in a New Zealand courtroom before, but Matthew Palmer explained that the legislation was clear: if an inconsistency between the bill of rights and the Crimes Act was found, Justice Collins was not only permitted to declare it, he was obliged to.

Lecretia was listening intently, stimulated by the legal discussion. This was rights law in practice, law making vital contact with the real world, and the courtroom bristled with energy. I followed as closely as I could, but the debate was clearly of greater interest to her, in the way that prior knowledge and learning expands an artwork's meaning for the observer.

Finally Andrew Butler drew attention to the deficiencies of palliative care. Lecretia's prognosis was grim, and, as Michael Ashby had testified, her perfectionist tendencies meant that palliative care was likely to exacerbate her psychological and emotional suffering. Dr Butler pointed out that the Crown's witnesses and Lecretia's witnesses all agreed, to varying levels, that palliative care was incapable of addressing all suffering. So what do we do for those people whom palliative care cannot help? Do we stand by and do nothing?

At the end of the day, Justice Collins adjourned the court, and we took a few moments in the jury room to collect ourselves. Lecretia was relaxed but exhausted as we wound our way to the car park beneath the building. At the exit, a number of photographers and camera crews were gathered, hoping to catch a glimpse of Lecretia in the passenger seat as she was driven away.

When we got home, we gathered in the living room and watched the news. Lecretia's case was a lead item. After an early dinner, she went to bed. I joined her later, putting my arms around her as she slept.

The next day Larry and I once again went to the court early, leaving Lecretia to sleep. The media were still out in force, and the public gallery was full once again. After Andrew Butler finished his arguments, the solicitor-general's team was invited to speak.

The solicitor-general's case was focused on the purpose and intent of the Crimes Act and the bill of rights. If the law was clarified in Lecretia's favour, he said, the effect would be equivalent to new legislation. It would destabilise the laws of homicide. He asserted that it was up to parliament to make such a decision, not the High Court. He could foresee a time when assisted dying was legal in New Zealand, but this was not the forum in which that change should be initiated.

The solicitor-general also suggested that a favourable ruling would place an administrative burden on the courts: would a judge have to preside over every petition for an assisted death? Would there be a number of these cases every year?

The difference in language was marked: Lecretia's lawyers talked about aid in dying, and assisted death, while the Crown's lawyers spoke of assisted suicide and euthanasia. In doing so, they asserted their arguments: for Lecretia's lawyers, what she was after was not suicide; for the Crown's lawyers, it was.

It caught my attention when the Crown mentioned the *Diagnostic and Statistical Manual of Mental Disorders*, the American Psychiatric Association's standard criteria used in diagnosing psychiatric disorders, which they noted did not make any distinction between a rational decision to die versus suicide. I knew that Allen Frances, the chairman of the taskforce that had compiled the DSM-IV, the edition which had been in use until 2013, had made several public statements in favour of assisted dying, and I flicked a text to Catherine Marks pointing this out. A rational decision to die is not a mental disorder, so it is no surprise it does not appear in the DSM.

The Crown also argued that Lecretia was vulnerable, in the sense that all human beings are vulnerable, and that laws designed to protect the vulnerable are there to protect all of us.

I was glad Lecretia had not arrived in time to hear this. She would have found this argument insulting. Meanwhile, Shirley had texted to say that Lecretia had only got up at around lunchtime, and it was unlikely she would make it into court today.

In the afternoon the Crown argued that Lecretia had access to the best palliative care available. If she were to suffer, well, that was part of life, and something we all experience. But I'd come to believe that humanity's role is to shape a better world. To ask, how can this be better? Society is defined by people who question the way things are and come up with new answers. Lecretia's case represented our quest for a more compassionate world, while the Crown was arguing that the existing one was good enough.

At home that evening, we watched the news together again. Lecretia had perked up a little, but was now confined to her armchair, moving from there to her wheelchair, and occasionally to a commode that had been provided by the hospice. She was deteriorating quite quickly, and the temozolomide was having no effect.

On the final day, the Crown finished its arguments and Andrew Butler received a right of reply. Lecretia was unable to attend again that morning. Andrew emphasised the fact that Lecretia faced a cruel choice between a lonely suicide and the possibility of a painful, drawn-out death. The right to life was really about quality of life, and autonomy. Obliging the terminally ill to live in order to protect the rights of others was a wrong-headed interpretation of the law, as no individual should be forced to suffer for the benefit of others.

The interveners finally got their chance to speak. Kate Davenport, speaking for the Voluntary Euthanasia Society, explained that, in effect, assisted dying was a form of treatment, a medical procedure, and that overseas jurisdictions had effectively legislated as such. If assisted dying was treatment, then the Crimes Act provisions should not apply—as treatment would be neither homicide nor assisted suicide.

Speaking for the Human Rights Commission, Matthew Palmer asserted that our bill of rights, though not explicitly stating a right to dignity, had dignity as one of its tenets, and that this had been demonstrated in various judgments made in New Zealand courts, including one or two made by Justice Collins. In 2013, in relation to a case regarding the withdrawal of treatment from a patient, Justice Collins had written that the purpose of section 9 of the bill of rights was to 'ensure that all persons are treated with respect and dignity and not subject to physical or psychological harm through cruel, degrading and disproportionately severe punishment or treatment'.

The word dignity did not appear in the bill of rights in that clause—in fact the word only appears once in the entire bill of rights, when referring to the treatment of someone arrested or detained—but in using that word Justice Collins acknowledged that it underpinned the document.

Victoria Casey, for the Care Alliance, described a hypothetical future in which the elderly and disabled were coerced to die, in what seemed to me to be an emotive narrative unsupported by facts or evidence. I was glad Lecretia didn't have to hear it.

Andrew was invited to respond briefly to the inter-veners. Once again he debated the nature of suicide. We heard the example of a soldier throwing himself on a grenade to save his comrades: a life-ending act, but suicide? If that was not suicide, then surely the definition of suicide was arguable? It was a fascinating day.

Shirley sent me a text to let me know that Lecretia was on her way. She arrived at around 3 pm, in time to hear some of Andrew's final statements. As he concluded, Justice Collins asked whether he thought that a recent amendment to the Crimes Act regarding vulnerability had some bearing on the case. The amendment had been recommended by the Law Commission. Justice Collins asked whether Lecretia had been involved with that amendment. She had not, but she smiled.

In closing, Justice Collins turned directly to Lecretia and thanked her for bringing an issue of such public importance to the courtroom. He said she had made a sizeable contribution to rights law in bringing the case. She smiled again, pleased to have been acknowledged.

He said: 'It is obviously a matter of extreme importance to you but also is extremely important to the way in which medicine and law are conducted in this country.' He complimented all the counsel for their submissions, saying that they had been exceptional and that it had been a privilege to listen to them. 'I only hope that my judgment will ultimately do justice to the quality of those submissions.'

In the jury room, Lecretia and her lawyers discussed the case. We felt confident. There was something in the way Justice Collins had finished the day that suggested things might go Lecretia's way. The Crown's arguments had been tested and in some cases exposed as wanting. There was an air of celebration. The case was over, and some good was certain to come of it. We believed that Lecretia's moral right to choose was absolute. The question was whether the law could be interpreted in a way that would allow it. We got the sense that Justice Collins might agree that it could.

Later that night, back at home, I wrote an email thanking the legal team at Russell McVeagh, which said in part:

Whichever way this case goes, there's no doubt that this will go down in case law as historic. As a team you have given Lecretia a great honour. I know that a lot of you worked long hours and weekends preparing submissions and evidence, reviewing arguments, interviewing experts and more, and I want to say how profoundly we appreciate all of that work. Andrew and Chris did an exemplary job with their oral submissions, and they were electrifying. I know the reason they were able to do that was because they were supported by a team of passionate solicitors who had worked tirelessly to prepare Lecretia's case. I hope that in working on my wife's case you have gained experience that will help you further your own careers, ambitions and lives, and that you found the case interesting and rewarding. It's the sort of thing Lecretia would have loved to have worked on herself, and the sort of case for which she took up law in the first place.

If Lecretia had lived in Belgium, or the Netherlands, or Oregon, she would have quietly inquired about being able to end her life if the pain and suffering was too much to bear. She would have made her decision in consultation with her family and her friends. If she'd decided to go ahead, she would have set a date, without fanfare and fuss, in a way that was consistent with how she had lived her life—privately, and with dignity. Her circumstances would have been uncontroversial: she would have been well within the boundaries of the law in any of those places. She would have had the death she wanted, either with or without assistance, surrounded by her loved ones. Her story would have been of no interest to the media at all.

But the laws in New Zealand forced her to confront the injustice of her situation. If she could have done it without media attention, she would have. If she'd managed to convince the minister of justice to initiate an investigation, working in tandem with the Law Commission, that would have been enough. If someone in parliament had launched a bill, that might have been enough too. She was a reluctant hero who believed the law was wrong and needed righting.

Lecretia never denied her privilege, and the fact she'd had a stellar career. She knew that she was fortunate, that on balance her life had turned out well. It kept her humble. But everything she had, she had worked for, a woman succeeding in a male-dominated profession. She had come from a poor family. While others in the law were second or third generation solicitors, went to private schools, had family connections, she had none of that. She was proud of her origins, and proud of her mother and father and the sacrifices they had made for her.

Lecretia was a law reformer, with a keen sense of justice and injustice. The case was framed around her, but her goal was to make circumstances like hers easier for others to bear. She wanted to make a difference. Given her story, and her expertise, she felt that she might just be able to do that.

Chapter 22

Discussion of the case remained intense in the days that followed. People were moved by Lecretia's plight, they could sympathise with her wishes, and up and down the country they were talking about end-of-life choice in a way they hadn't before. The topic was discussed at dinner tables and in pubs and restaurants around the country. Shouldn't we have a choice about how we die? Shouldn't we have some say about our final moments? What is the benefit of suffering at the end of life?

Lecretia's case was generating interest overseas, too. If the judge found in her favour it would become a landmark case. It was important to me that the decision went her way. I wanted her to change the world. I wanted her to never be forgotten. After everything she'd put herself through to make the case possible, she deserved nothing less.

Her health was declining rapidly. The day after the case, she had trouble getting out of bed. She was brought into the lounge to sit in her armchair, where I read to her some of the published debate that followed the case. Catherine Marks called and told me that the word through the legal grapevine was that the Crown felt that they'd lost. This was a boost for Lecretia and me.

On Friday, two days after the case, it was more difficult to get Lecretia out of bed. She wasn't able to bend her body at all. The hospital had sent out a hoist to our house, and it arrived that morning, a device the size of a refrigerator. Apparently we were to put Lecretia into a sling and to move her around with this thing, but there was no way to get her into it. We called the hospice and a palliative care doctor and a nurse came to visit Lecretia at lunchtime. They took a quick look at her and decided that what she needed was a hospital bed. We called the hospital, and were told a bed would be delivered that afternoon.

It never arrived. Lecretia was fine in the bed in the bedroom, but she wanted to be out in the lounge, with us around her, a part of the events of the day. She lay in her armchair, which was fully reclined, but her body was as stiff as a board, her posterior barely touching the armchair cushion, with most of the pressure on her neck and the backs of her legs. She began to have trouble swallowing, and would frequently choke when given water. She was lucid occasionally, but drifted in and out of a sort of fugue.

Lecretia had been bright and awake just a few days earlier, but it was now apparent that she was possibly beyond the point of competence. Could consent be freely given in this situation? Whatever the judgment was, would she still be in a state to make a decision about her own life? Would her advance directive apply? Would I have to make the call about when her life no longer had quality? I tried to imagine what the healthy Lecretia would make of this, if she could be here, watching herself in this state. Would she regard her life, at this point, as essentially over? Would the Lecretia of the past decide that the Lecretia of the present had lived as much as she needed to? I never arrived at an answer.

The hospital got in touch on Saturday morning, and with the help of a district nurse pulling strings, we arranged to pick up a proper patient's bed. Lecretia's friend Angela brought her SUV. We put the bed in the back and took it home. It took a while to put together, but now we could raise and lower each half of the bed to bring Lecretia into a comfortable sitting position.

We covered Lecretia with blankets and a quilt that a colleague from the Law Commission had made her. Ferdinand was unsure of the bed at first, but after circling it a few times he gathered the courage to launch himself onto it. He curled up at Lecretia's feet, and every so often would climb up her body, resting on her chest and pushing his face against hers. She smiled whenever he did so.

Shirley had had some more feijoas delivered from Tauranga—the soft fruit was easy for Lecretia to eat. Shirley scooped the flesh out with a teaspoon and fed it to Lecretia, who insisted that her mother keep the spoonfuls coming.

I sat beside her and retraced our memories. I described our wedding, and our holidays in the Cook Islands and Argentina and Morocco, lingering on the scenes I knew she would appreciate, the times we'd lain on beaches together, or swum in a lagoon, recalling the salty taste of the ocean and the smell of sunscreen and the feeling of the warm sand, the blue sky, and the sounds of strange birds. These memories seemed to make her happy.

Lecretia spoke occasionally. At one point she looked directly at me and said, 'Let's go—I want to get in the car.'

'Where do you want to go?'

'Anywhere. Let's go.'

'We need to decide where we're going.'

'I don't care,' she said. 'I need to get out of here.'

Did she imagine that her illness was tied to this house, this room, this bed, that it was something she could cast off and walk away from? I wished that were true. I would have taken her anywhere if that were true.

Every few hours she had a seizure. This was new. Her body quaked, her leg hammering against the air mattress and her foot against the end of the bed. Her mother or I would gently embrace her until it stopped. It was clear to us both that some Rubicon had been crossed. Lecretia had not suffered seizures since her fall in the first year of her illness. They had been kept in check by medication that was no longer working.

By Sunday we had given up trying to feed Lecretia solid foods. We stuck to small amounts of soup and liquids, which she ate without complaint.

On Monday, I called Catherine Marks, telling her that Lecretia had entered a precipitous decline. Was there any way to let the judge know? She promised to contact the court and to get back to us. The nurses visited, and Lecretia was turned and washed in her bed. She was now in adult diapers, unable to get out of bed even with assistance.

It was incredible to me that my wife had been in a courtroom barely five days prior. It was as though she had used up all her strength to be there, and now she was letting her illness take its inexorable toll. It was creeping through her like a thick fog; each day more of it would obscure her essence. I was watching my wife die.

On Tuesday we received word that Justice Collins was now aware of Lecretia's deterioration. He asked, very kindly, whether she would like to receive an interim judgment, which would tell her whether she would be able to access aid in dying services under current New Zealand law. If the judge ruled that Lecretia's doctor would not risk prosecution for helping her to die, Lecretia would have her choice. Lecretia agreed to receive the interim judgment.

The interim judgment was delivered to Russell McVeagh on the afternoon of Tuesday 2 June. Catherine forwarded it to me. Sadly, and to my surprise, Justice Collins had ruled that a physician helping Lecretia to die in accordance with her wishes would continue to risk prosecution. He had answered the first of Lecretia's questions. Did she have a choice about whether she could legally seek assistance from a doctor to die? She did not. Lecretia's second question—whether her rights and fundamental freedoms were infringed by New Zealand law—remained unanswered. Justice Collins said that he would give his full reasoning in his judgment, due later in the week. But he had denied Lecretia her choice. She would die in whatever way it happened.

Looking at Lecretia then, at the strength and courage with which she was enduring her decline, I suspected that she would have rejected assisted dying as an option. So why go to all this trouble?

Because choices matter. Choices are what make us human, and not slaves. Without choices, we don't have free will. We are held hostage. And when you're dying, that last choice is a gift. An acknowledgment that, when it comes to your own body, you have the final say.

That day she spent a lot of the time unconscious, unable to speak. She could barely open her one good eye. In the evening I relayed Justice Collins' decision to her. I explained she would not be able to seek assistance to die, but that her mother and I would do everything we could to make her comfortable and pain free, and that we would accede to the wishes she had laid out in her advance directive in accordance with the law.

Lecretia listened to me as I explained. She could not speak, but she was able to share her feelings through her eyes and her expression. There was no mistaking her response. She was hurt and disappointed. She fixed me with a stare, as if to say: *Isn't this my body? My life?* Her breath slowed. She turned her head away. I wondered whether I should have been telling her any of this. Her reaction broke my heart.

I explained that the judge had not yet released his decision about whether her rights were infringed by current law. She turned to me again and looked at me with determination. A rights breach was the basis of the rulings in Canada and South Africa. It was still possible one might be found here. She knew a ruling in her favour could motivate our parliament to act, which in turn could benefit so many others who might find themselves in a state like hers.

On Wednesday, Lecretia was almost totally unresponsive. Her eyes remained closed and she hardly moved. She was not eating and she was barely drinking. A pump gave her a steady supply of anti-seizure medication and a very low dose of morphine. Lecretia had begun to starve herself to death, and in accordance with her wishes we did not intervene, nor allow her doctors to do so.

I talked to her but she rarely gave me any indication she could hear me. I held her hand and sat with her. The bed was close to the window. Outside there was a cherry tree whose leaves had yellowed and begun to fall. She could not see it, but it was beautiful and I described it to her, and the tuis and blackbirds nestled in its branches.

She looked so peaceful that it was almost as if she was in a deep sleep. It seemed as if, were she to awaken, her eyes would open brightly and she would be restored. My head knew this wouldn't happen, but my heart still wished it to be true.

When I looked at Lecretia, I saw no suffering, no lack of dignity. I saw a strong, beautiful woman who was facing death with grace and strength. I didn't know whether suffering and indignity were still to come, or whether she was suffering and she was unable to tell me.

Nevertheless, I did not feel that my view, or anyone else's, should stand in the way of Lecretia's choice to live or die on her terms. As her husband, I chose to honour her as a human being with her own free will and her own choices. I honoured her as my equal, even in these circumstances. That is respect. That is dignity. That is love.

The final judgment arrived on Thursday. We had received it in advance of the media, who would not have it for another twenty-four hours. It was a fifty-five-page document. Justice Collins had written it in a mere seven days. It was a herculean effort on his part.

I read it and despaired. Not only had he not declared that a doctor would not be prosecuted under the Crimes Act, but he failed to find an inconsistency with the bill of rights. It was heartbreaking. All that work, all of that evidence, for nothing.

But, re-reading it, I found glimmers of hope. He called Lecretia's request a rational and intellectually rigorous response to her circumstances. He declared that the ethical questions her case had raised were far from settled, and neither side had a claim to absolute truth. He declared that Lecretia was not vulnerable, and not coerced, and added:

> Palliative care cannot necessarily provide relief from suffering in all cases. The limits of palliative care were explained by Ms Seales' principal oncologist, experts who provided evidence in support of Ms Seales' case and some of the experts relied upon by the attorney-general.
>
> Second, experts who gave evidence in support of the case brought by Ms Seales and some of the experts who supported the position adopted by the attorney-general agreed that pain is highly subjective. This means that Ms Seales' perception of her pain is unimpeachable.
>
> Third, Ms Seales' circumstances are such that palliative care may not ameliorate her physical pain. I have reached this conclusion by relying primarily on the evidence of the experts who have given evidence on behalf of Ms Seales because they tailored their evidence to her particular circumstances.
>
> Fourth, many of the experts, including those relied upon by the attorney-general, accept that palliative care may not be able to address Ms Seales' psychological and emotional suffering.

It was an admission that there are some whom palliative care cannot reach, and that the aims of palliative care were not sufficient in themselves to support a prohibition on assisted dying.

This was further supported when Justice Collins accepted the evidence from the Canadian historian Dr Weaver that there were those in New Zealand who kill themselves in order to avoid the worst of their illnesses. It prompted an obvious question: would they kill themselves in that way if assisted dying were available?

Despite taking on board the ethical concerns of the witnesses for the defence, Justice Collins felt that Lecretia's circumstances resonated more with the experiences of those doctors who had asserted that patients in such circumstances feel empowered and reassured knowing that they can choose the time and surrounding circumstances of their demise.

He also said Lecretia had consistently maintained that she was not vulnerable in any sense, and noted:

> She says that, notwithstanding her medical condi-tion, her wishes have been carefully considered and reasoned. Ms Seales' self-assessment that she is not vulnerable is endorsed by her doctor, who has consistently said Ms Seales is pursuing her requests in a positive, rational manner without showing any

signs of depression or lack of full appreciation of her circumstances. Ms Seales' statement of her belief that she is not vulnerable must be respected. Ms Seales' application for the declarations she seeks is a rational and intellectually rigorous response to her circumstances.

Nonetheless he was unable to rule in Lecretia's favour. On the question of consent to be assisted to die, he found that the provisions prohibiting it had their basis in UK law, where 'the interest of the state in preserving life overrides the otherwise all-powerful interest of patient autonomy'. In summary, he said:

> In reaching this conclusion, I emphasise that I have applied a legal analysis. By focusing upon the law it may appear that I am indifferent to Ms Seales' plight. Nothing could be further from the truth. I fully acknowledge that the consequences of the law against assisting suicide as it currently stands are extremely distressing for Ms Seales and that she is suffering because that law does not accommodate her right to dignity and personal autonomy.
>
> Although Ms Seales has not obtained the outcomes she sought, she has selflessly provided a forum to clarify important aspects of New Zealand law. The complex legal, philosophical, moral and

clinical issues raised by Ms Seales' proceedings can only be addressed by parliament passing legislation to amend the effect of the Crimes Act. I appreciate parliament has shown little desire to engage in these issues. The three private members' bills that have attempted to address the broad issues raised by Ms Seales' proceeding gained little legislative traction. However, the fact that parliament has not been willing to address the issues raised by Ms Seales' proceeding does not provide me with a licence to depart from the constitutional role of judges in New Zealand.

On reading the judgment, I got the sense that Justice Collins knew the right answer but hadn't found a way to give Lecretia the choice she wanted through the law as it was written. It was almost as if he'd started out one way, got into the legal analysis, and changed his mind. Though the judgment was measured and reasonable in tone, there was the unmistakable implication that this was something our parliament had to deal with, and that it had been remiss in its failure to do so.

After reviewing the judgment, I read as much of it to Lecretia as I could bear. I don't know whether she heard it. She was breathing heavily, her eyes were closed, and every so often she would let out a soft groan. Was this to be her final memory? That she'd failed to achieve what she had fought for? It seemed cruel to do that to her—and yet it felt important for her to know. What was happening was wrong, but it was the law.

On Thursday afternoon, Lecretia was completely unconscious, breathing slowly, the slightest gurgle in the back of her throat.

A press conference was scheduled for Friday in response to Justice Collins' ruling. I sat beside Lecretia as I began to compose our statement. Every so often I'd hold her hand. At about 9 pm I went to bed. I was exhausted. But I was woken at about 11 pm by Larry. 'Matt,' he said, 'I think something's happening—you'd better wake up.'

I came out to the lounge and there was no doubt things had changed. Lecretia's eyes were open and there was a loud gurgle in her throat, much louder than before. The volume of it filled the room, a thick, crackling rattle. I called the nurse at the hospital and asked what to do. She said this was normal. 'Has no one told you what to expect?' She advised we give Lecretia Buscopan. I prepared the syringe and gave her some.

It didn't appear to make much difference. Shirley, Larry and I sat beside the bed as Lecretia continued to struggle for breath. Her eyes remained open. She looked at me, at her father and at her mother, and we said things like

'It's okay, Lecretia' and 'You're okay' and 'We're with you and we love you' and 'Matt's here, Mum's here, Dad's here' and 'We love you, Lecretia.'

I could hear that the liquid in Lecretia's throat was thickening. Her breath stopped a couple of times. She'd exhale and hold, and then suddenly inhale sharply. I moved her head slightly to make her comfortable and a long ribbon of liquid snaked from her mouth and down her front, white like sunscreen.

In those moments I remember feeling helpless. I wanted to do something for Lecretia, to help her to breathe better, or, yes, to help her on her way, but neither Shirley nor Larry nor I did anything. We watched helplessly as Lecretia fought to breathe, her eyes open, taking us in, and she drowned. It took an hour and a half. Then she didn't breathe again.

'She's gone,' Larry said, his voice cracking.

I just held her hand and wept, while her parents wept beside me.

My wife was so brave. She did not complain, cry out, lash out, moan, scream, or cry. She just struggled for breath, and then she died.

And even now I think: what could we have done differently? Should I have tilted her head further to clear more of the fluids in her throat? Should I have drugged her up on more morphine, the thing she didn't want and which didn't seem to work anyway? How much pain was she in? How much had she suffered? Was she afraid? She couldn't speak to tell us how she was feeling, but she opened her other eye after it had been closed for so long. When I think of the reasons why eyes widen—fear, surprise, pain—I become terrified of what she might have felt in her final moments. She wanted a loving goodbye. I guess she got as close to that as she could hope for within the law. But it wasn't neat and tidy. It wasn't painless. It would be terrifying to struggle for breath for an hour and a half. I don't think the fact you're dying would change that. I think it would make it worse.

If I've reconciled myself to the way Lecretia died, the drowning, it's because I've taken comfort in the fact that it was over relatively quickly. But those last few hours—if she'd had the choice, and could have said so—would she have wanted to live them? Those last few hours felt unkind and unnecessary. They were empty of meaning. There was only pain and sorrow and wishing that it would be over.

After she died, I looked at her. Her body was still, her face fixed in its expression. I put my thumb on her eyelids and closed each like a window-shade. I put my hand under her chin, and closed her mouth. It stayed shut. Her hand, which I held, started to cool. It was over.

Chapter 23

I COULDN'T SLEEP of course. I began calling people. Some of them burst into tears over the phone. No one was surprised that it had happened, though some were surprised that it had happened so soon.

I wasn't crying. I was done crying for now. I wrote a media release and sent the news out: *On Friday 5 June 2015, at 12.35 am, Lecretia Seales, the forty-two-year-old Wellington lawyer with terminal brain cancer, died of natural causes ... Ms Seales' death came just hours after her family and lawyers received Justice Collins' full judgment. The judge has embargoed his decision until 15.00 hours today.*

We knew what the judgment was, even if the public didn't. In a few hours I would have to stand in front of the media and tell them that Lecretia had not got the judgment she sought.

Natural causes. It wasn't quite right. Lecretia's body had turned against her. The soft machinery inside her head had slipped a gear and lost control. It didn't feel natural.

But I needed to signal that she hadn't been helped. I didn't want that to be an open question. I wanted people to be sad that she died, not wonder whether she had been assisted. I wanted the question in people's minds to be: *What was Justice Collins' ruling?* Not whether her doctor had helped her to die.

A media briefing was scheduled for 3 pm. I finalised my statement. I knew we had to create the biggest impact we could, to stick the spurs deep into the government's flank and goad them to action. With the judgment not going our way, it was our last chance. Someone brought me in lunch and a glass of whisky. I didn't touch either. I walked into the briefing room to almost total silence, the only sound the snapping of cameras and barely perceptible scribble of pens on notebooks, and gave them the news that Lecretia had died, expressing my disappointment at Justice Collins' ruling.

It took fifteen minutes to read through my statement. There was no applause, just an uncomfortable silence. I folded up the paper, put it back in my pocket, and then turned towards the door and walked out. The only sound I could hear was the click of camera shutters and the clack of my shoes on the parquet floor as I left.

In the days that followed, I felt the intense scrutiny of the country and the world on us. The delivery of the judgment and my wife's passing were like a great rock thrown into water, sending waves rippling outward. At the crest of every ripple, people were making their own judgments, asking their own questions, drawing conclusions. I understood then that for many people the most significant day in my wife's short life was her last day. Her wedding day, her graduation, her first steps: these were the special memories of a select few. Most would remember Lecretia for the day she died, and the judgment she received on that day. And I wasn't really prepared for that. I wasn't prepared for people to see my wife's life as a tragedy. Because so much of it wasn't.

After Lecretia died, on the day the High Court ruled against her right to choose how her life ended, I was afraid that everything about her would be reduced to this single event. I wanted people to know how truly special she was, and how much of her life was a love story, and how much she achieved. I wanted all the sadness to be an epilogue, and not the climax.

We had called a funeral home. I'd picked one at random. Keith, the funeral director, arrived midmorning with a colleague. He was a tall man with grey hair and a slate-blue suit and he looked the part. He was friendly but not too friendly. His voice was clear but only as loud as it needed to be. There were decisions: What casket would Lecretia like? What flowers would she want? Had we thought about music?

Keith took Lecretia's body away. They covered her with a sheet and wheeled her out on a gurney, up our switchback pathway to the main road where the hearse was parked. It was a grey day and the sky was concrete. It bothered me that cars were driving past as we came out to the road. It all bothered me. None of it made any sense. The funeral home staff were dressed in grey suits and they weren't smiling and I felt like I would have punched them if they did. I watched as the hearse pulled away from the curb. I didn't want my wife to leave that way. I didn't want her to leave at all.

To keep busy I moved almost everything from the hospital up to our garage for collection. The hoist, the bed. I kept the electric armchair in the house and I sat in it, pushing the button to make the footrest come up. I drank some beer. Someone brought dinner over for us. We ate it and one of Lecretia's friends organised a roster for people to bring us meals. We were showered with kindness.

Flowers began arriving, big bouquets of lilies and chrysanthemums, orchids in pots, buckets of hyacinths and hydrangeas. We arranged them in our living room in front of the fireplace. And cards too, from people Lecretia knew well and others she hadn't seen in years. Cards that offered condolences to me, or to her parents, or to her parents and siblings, or to all of us. They were arranged on the mantelpiece—where we used to put birthday cards and Christmas cards—but there were too many cards, and they started piling up on the dining room table, along with letters and other gifts too. I kept having to make new piles as the existing ones spilled over onto the floor. I asked Andrew, Kat's husband, to keep a record, so I could write back to all of these people.

The undertaker brought Lecretia back to the house in the rosewood coffin that we'd selected for her. We had to carry the coffin back down the switchback path. It took six of us, and it was heavy. We went slowly, careful not to scratch the beautiful varnished surface. Once we had it safely down the path, the coffin was wheeled into the house on a special stainless-steel trolley. Somewhere in the world there is a company that makes these things, I thought. There is someone who dreamt this up. How long,

I wondered, stupidly, had the inventor waited before being carried out by their own invention?

The coffin was brought into the living room and arranged in exactly the spot where Lecretia had last been alive in her bed. The staff loosened the screws and lifted the lid of the casket, and leaned it against a nearby wall. Lecretia's name was engraved on a silver nameplate on the lid. I checked the spelling as it was the thing I was most nervous about. People always got it wrong.

In her coffin Lecretia was wearing the green dress we'd chosen for her. I was upset that strangers had dressed her. I didn't want to think about it too much. At her waist, her left hand was folded over her right, so that her wedding ring was visible. I put my hand on her hand and it was cold: colder than it had ever been. Her fingers felt like a porcelain doll's. I suppose, if not for the embalmer's work, they would have been the colour of a porcelain doll's too. They were beautiful.

But her face and neck looked wrong. Her head was too low, and her neck was shorter than the elegant neck I remembered, and where the neck and chest met, her skin had gathered in three narrow pleats. She didn't carry herself that way. She didn't sleep that way. On her head was one of her hairpieces, but it was arranged strangely.

'How does she look?' asked the director.

'Fine. Good,' I lied. I didn't want them to take her away again. I didn't want them to touch her again.

'You can rearrange her if you want. It's safe to move her if you're gentle.'

'Okay.'

People began arriving. Some didn't want to look at her. Some took a brief glance; others leaned over her coffin and wept. People cry differently. Some cry with their mouths and noses. Some cry from deep in their chest and shudder as they breathe. Some don't appear to cry at all. Their face is a mask and then they hold you and you feel them crying. And the way they hold you is different from the way you're held by a lover. They hold their arms out like a child, or like you're a child, and the arms go around you, and their head is rested on your shoulder, and you feel them shake in your chest and on your cheek.

A lover is held with one arm around the shoulder and one around the waist, or both around the waist. You pull each other together, and every inch of you is connected from chest to thigh, or you pull your chest back, just a little, so you can face each other, and smile, and kiss. I was being held like a child and I wanted to be held by a lover. I wanted to be held by my wife. I wanted everyone to leave so I could climb in that coffin with her and hold her. And maybe I would have, if I wasn't scared the trolley would break or that I would damage her. She looked so fragile, my porcelain doll, and the trolley was such a flimsy-looking thing.

After a few hours I removed her hairpiece. I took her head and I lifted it slightly, back into the coffin, smoothing away those three offensive pleats in the paper-thin skin of her neck. She still looked different, but she was more recognisably my wife. She looked so much better without the hairpiece. You couldn't see where her hair had thinned from the radiotherapy, where the scar from her surgery wound around her scalp like the loop of an omega. She looked well, almost, as though she'd gone to the hairdresser to trim the last of her beautiful chestnut hair, leaving only a pixie cut.

We spent four days and evenings in the house with Lecretia at rest in her coffin. At night I would put the lid of the coffin down, and in the morning I would take it off again. It was good to have her in the house, to have the chance to say goodbye. Alone in the house with her, I sat beside the coffin and told her everything. Everything I loved about her, everything I was guilty about, the mistakes I'd made, the deep regret at ever having hurt her feelings, even for a moment. I thought back to that incident where I hadn't called her after getting drunk with friends, and how hurt she had been, and the expression on her face, and how I could never take that back, that it and all the other times like it were now fixed in amber and she could no longer hear me say sorry. That was the hardest part: that she'd ever been hurt or suffered at all, and that I had been the cause of any of it. She was such a good person, and she didn't get the things she deserved: kids and a long life.

The funeral was held at Old St Paul's cathedral in Thorndon. It was a beautiful service. I spoke, along with Lecretia's mother and father, her sister Kat, and her friend Angela. Sir Geoffrey Palmer gave a wonderful speech about Lecretia's skill as a lawyer, and another former colleague from the Law Commission, Professor John Burrows QC, spoke about how much fun Lecretia was to work with, and how she had no qualms about telling him when she thought he was wrong about something.

At the end of the service, I played a video that Lecretia had recorded the weekend before she went into surgery. She was healthy and whole, and spoke about how much she'd enjoyed her life and how lucky she felt to have had everything she had. Even though the video was four years old, Lecretia's attitude had not changed since then—she remained grateful and joyous right up until the end. The words she said on the video could have been said only a week ago.

After the eulogies, I gathered with the other pallbearers and we carried Lecretia's coffin out to the waiting hearse. The four or five hundred guests followed and assembled outside the church. The hearse drove away. Among all those friends and family I felt very alone.

Chapter 24

IT FEELS LIKE I'm moving through a different world now. It's adjacent to the old one, but it's a world in which Lecretia does not exist, and for that reason it seems strange and foreign. The rules for me are different now, and I find it hard to embrace them. I want to wish this strange new world away and return to the old one with all its love and kindness. But Lecretia is still here. Over time the atoms of her body will disperse, becoming part of the earth, of trees, of animals, of flowers. Those atoms, before they coalesced into the miracle she was, resided in fish and dinosaurs and sabre-toothed tigers. The building blocks of life have their permanence in atoms, and the miracle of consciousness is like a spark thrown off by the flick of flint against the dull edge of the periodic table. And I am so grateful that I saw Lecretia's moment burn so brightly. I miss her terribly.

In the days and weeks and months that followed Lecretia's death and funeral, the issue of assisted dying was widely debated. A petition asking parliament to investigate public attitudes to assisted dying attracted thousands of signatures. It became the trigger for a select committee to canvass public opinion and explore whether the law should be changed. The select committee received over 19,000 submissions and is likely to deliver a report in 2017.

Once the petition was handed in, I stuck around home for a few weeks, not working. Her memory was still overwhelming for me. I read books, and people sent me their stories, which was both a comfort and very tough too. It was overwhelming to hear some of the things other people had gone through when losing someone. The dirty little secret of palliative care is that some people have atrocious experiences, not through any fault of the carers, more as a result of their illnesses, but afterwards they're not around to complain about it, and their families are so upset that they keep quiet as they don't want to relive the memory. They just smoulder in anger and pray and hope the same thing doesn't happen to them when it's their turn.

I had to get away. In July I booked flights to go overseas and I spent two months travelling. I went on a cruise in the Baltic Sea, explored Denmark and Iceland, and experienced the sights and sounds of New York for the first time. I backpacked for five weeks in Mexico in August and September. I met a woman there, a wonderful lady, and spent two weeks living with her in Mexico City. Part of me wanted to give up on my ties to New Zealand and stay in Mexico, with its food and its people and this woman who cared for me a great deal, who through her kindness and affection was mending my heart. Being in a different culture and using a different language was a break from a reality that had been so difficult for so long, as though I had escaped to another life.

When I finally came home again, I picked up my bags at the airport and my mother and sister collected me. They drove me back to my place. All the ramps we'd put in for Lecretia's wheelchair had gone. My mum and sister wanted to come in, but I didn't want them to. I entered the house alone, for the first time in months, hoping my absence had exorcised it of memory. But it had not. Things came flooding back. Our photographs were still arrayed on the table, every object told a story, and those stories all led back to Lecretia. I felt the full force of her presence, and her absence. All those months of numbness dropped away and I felt the magnitude of what I'd lost. And I had lost everything I cared about.

It was the middle of the afternoon, and yet I cried myself to sleep.

Chapter 25

SHORTLY BEFORE CHRISTMAS, I was contacted by the *New Zealand Herald*. The *Herald* is the most widely read newspaper in the country, and it had decided to make Lecretia New Zealander of the Year. I was stunned. I was immensely proud of my wife.

Lecretia would have been embarrassed by it, but I think, underneath it all, a little proud, too. She did devote her life to helping others, though in a less obvious way: through law and policy advice that benefited all New Zealanders. There are many others who do such work, and it was only because of Lecretia's case that anyone was aware of her other contributions over the years. But to have her recognised was a balm for me. I couldn't bear the idea of her being forgotten. People would know who she was and what she did.

A few days after the announcement, I was at home contemplating my options for Christmas. I didn't know what to do. I hadn't spent a family Christmas with my mother or my father for years. My sister Natalie's son Thomas was growing up. But so was Rafferty, Jeremy and Kate's son, and Lecretia and I adored him so much that I wanted to see him too.

In the end I booked flights to Tauranga the day before Christmas Eve, and Larry picked me up at the airport. There were grey skies over the Bay of Plenty as we drove home, talking about everything that had happened that year. I brought Larry up to date with the petition and the select committee and he responded appreciatively, but I sensed his continuing sorrow at his daughter's loss, and how my presence was just another reminder of the fact that she was gone.

When I stayed with Lecretia's parents, I slept in her bedroom at the back of the house. Some of her clothes and hats still hung on a stand, and the plush animals she'd never discarded were piled high in a corner of the room: bears and dogs and rabbits. On her neatly ordered bookshelf you could track her reading: from Enid Blyton through to Sweet Valley High and teenage romances, Stephen King and the racier Jilly Cooper. There were faded cookbooks, and then her law textbooks, serious and heavy tomes. Outside her window the sun was setting over trees and bushes and the peaked roofs cresting through the canopy, and orange light filled the room.

I lay on the bed that I'd shared with her over many Christmases. It was small: the room couldn't fit more than a double mattress. I recalled how the heat of the Tauranga summer made sleeping in that room uncomfortable, and that I would often wake and despite the heat I would reach for her and hold her and listen to her breathing with my arms curled around her stomach. I'd rest my head on the smooth part of her back below her shoulders, my knees tucked up under her thighs. If we were both awake, I would flirt with her and tease her, but she didn't want her parents, sleeping in the next room, to hear us. Instead we'd quietly kiss and hold each other. Her kisses were warm and sweet.

On Christmas morning I would wait for her to wake up and gleefully go to the door to collect our Christmas stockings. With the joy of a little girl, she'd pull out the gifts for herself that she'd mostly already chosen with her mother. It was the ritual she liked, the joy of being alive, and the prospect of a day with her entire family, with food and drink and laughter and gift-giving and long afternoon naps.

Alone on Lecretia's bed, I felt aggrieved. Here a young girl slept, and woke, and got ready for school. She talked on the phone with her friends. At night, her dreams and hopes took shape in this room, and she decided to become a lawyer. She came home from university for the holidays, bringing her textbooks with her, piling them up on the shelves. She studied the law and wanted to make a difference. How many sunsets had she seen from the same window I was looking out now? What did she think about, as she watched the sun go down?

We live in an unjust world. People die too young. Some people don't have children. Some people get cancer. Some people don't have enough to eat. Some people are born into bad families, bad towns, bad countries. And choices—choices are how we deal with all that. We choose to be happy without kids, we choose to face illnesses like cancer and live our lives to the fullest, while we can. We choose to get up in the morning and go to work. We choose to eat. We choose to walk away from the bad things in our lives and try to do good, try to add a little kindness to the world, to drive out the hurt and the suffering. And the law is how we try to make it all just. We name and prosecute crimes to prevent others from hurting us. We regulate to make trade and commerce fair. We litigate to right wrongs, and we negotiate contracts to protect each other from surprises and the sharp edges of the spinning dice that sever every tether.

It's tempting to end this neatly. To tie it up with a little bow and some sort of resolution. But it hasn't ended. It won't end until the choice that Lecretia was denied is the right of every terminally ill person. When Lecretia was denied her final choice, she was denied her humanity: she became a patient, a sufferer, not a competent human being able to express her free will. Lecretia decided to love life even as it denied her children, decided to celebrate her life with cancer rather than despair of it, decided to speak out and became a hero to others, to her family, and to me. She taught me that we should have choices right until the end. It was Lecretia's last hope that one of these days we all will.

ACKNOWLEDGMENTS

This book couldn't have been written without the support and help of a great many people. I have a huge amount of gratitude for those who were there with Lecretia through her illness and her court case, as their actions had a direct impact on this story and gave it its shape.

Firstly I wish to thank Lecretia's family. Larry and Shirley were hugely supportive during Lecretia's illness, making incredible sacrifices to help us both, and they continued to support me after Lecretia passed away. They are like another set of parents to me. Lecretia's brother Jeremy and her sister Kat and their partners have never stopped treating me like part of their family, even if the person who brought us together is no longer with us. Lecretia's extended family of aunts, uncles and cousins are some of the nicest people I have ever met, and their support through my grief has been a tremendous help in getting me through the darkest period of my life.

My parents Robin and Catherine and their spouses, my sister Natalie and her husband Adrian and my brother Mike all helped me at one time or another when I needed it, keeping me on the straight and narrow before I met Lecretia and expressing relief when I found her.

I am grateful too to Lecretia's employers at the Law Commission, Sir Grant Hammond, Peter Boshier, Geoff McLay, Wayne Mapp and Roland Daysh, who allowed Lecretia to keep her job for as long as she did, giving her the latitude to continue her work as her illness progressed to its final stages. I also wish to thank the many staff of the Law Commission, too numerous to be named, who continued to include Lecretia in their ukulele orchestra performances, even when all she could do was sing.

I am grateful for the sensitivity and respect that Lecretia's story was treated with by most of the media. Rebecca Macfie, Hagen Hopkins and Pamela Stirling were the first to realise the strength of Lecretia's story when they covered it in the *Listener*, and they continued to follow it as it developed. Rebecca Macfie's pieces for the *Listener* are still the most in-depth journalism on who Lecretia was and the claims she made before the High Court. For another account of the circumstances leading up to the court case and the days that followed, Rebecca's articles are an invaluable resource.

Janet McIntyre and Carolyne Meng-Yee's story for *Sunday* introduced Lecretia to the wider public, and gave the greatest spur to her campaign that one could hope for. It is through their efforts and the work of the *Sunday* team that Lecretia became a household name, and their story is why many people still talk about her today.

Thank you also to the many other journalists and reporters who covered Lecretia's story over the months preceding and following her hearing. Though there are a great many, in particular I recall the coverage of Graham Adams, Michele A'Court, Emma Alberici, Jess Berentson-Shaw, Nick Bond, Emily Cooper, Mark Cubey, Jennifer Dann, Andrew Dickens, Rod Emmerson, David Farrar, Tim Fookes, Duncan Garner, Andrew Geddis, Renée Graham, Paul Henry, Kim Hill, Mike Hosking, Nicholas Jones, Katie Kenny, Zoë Lawton, Sharon Lundy, Kerre McIvor, Rebecca Quilliam, Kathryn Ryan, Mark Sainsbury, Jared Savage, Geoff Simmons, Rachel Smalley, Alastair Thompson, Chris Trotter, Nick Walker and John Weekes, though there were many, many others and I profusely apologise to those I might have missed.

I must make special mention of Miriyana Alexander and Phil Taylor, who supported Lecretia being named New Zealander of the Year by the *New Zealand Herald*. After an incredibly challenging year, I could not have hoped for a better tribute to my late wife.

I am especially thankful to Susanna Andrew and Jolisa Gracewood for their early support of the Lecretia's Choice blog, and their decision to include excerpts from it in *Tell You What: Great New Zealand Nonfiction 2016*. That endorsement of my writing gave me the courage to pursue the publication of this book, and they are part of the reason you now find it in your hands.

Similarly, I am grateful for the generous advice of many in the New Zealand publishing industry, including Fergus Barrowman, Sam Elworthy, Rachael King, Elizabeth Knox, Finlay Macdonald, Debra Millar, Emily Perkins and Mary Varnham, who each offered invaluable insights on how to best publish Lecretia's story.

Text Publishing have been fantastic to work with, and I am grateful to publisher Michael Heyward for seeing the potential in Lecretia's story, and everyone at Text including Léa Antigny, Anne Beilby, W. H. Chong, Alice Cottrell, Elizabeth Cowell, Alaina Gougoulis, Jessica Horrocks, Jane Novak, Jane Pearson and Kirsty Wilson. They have all worked tirelessly to make sure I have written the best book I possibly could. I am particularly grateful for the patient work of Elizabeth, with whom I tussled over edits for the last few months.

Thank you also to Steven Price, who took time from paternity leave to review this book and provide invaluable legal advice. This book is much stronger for his input.

The book would also not have been possible without the generous support of my employer, Xero. I am grateful to Rod Drury, Alastair Grigg, Angus Norton, Duncan

Ritchie and Graham Shaw, whose personal championing of me inside and outside of work made the writing of this book possible. Bradley Scott and Andrew Tokeley also deserve to be thanked for the kindness and patience they showed me during Lecretia's illness.

Although neither Lecretia nor I were members of the Voluntary Euthanasia Society of New Zealand, this did not deter them from providing support and help in Lecretia's case. Jack Havill, Carole Sweney, Faye Clark, Eileen Howarth and Philip Patston have greatly assisted over the last few months in keeping Lecretia's story alive. And thank you also to Kate Davenport, who ably represented their views in the courtroom.

I must also mention those who took the time out of their busy lives to prepare affidavits for Lecretia's case: Dr Michael Ashby, Dr Linda Ganzini, Associate Professor Colin Gavaghan, Dr David Grube, Dr Jack Havill, Dr Eric Kress, Dr Phillipa Malpas, Dr Katherine Morris, Dr Rajesh Munglani, Professor Richard Glynn Owens, Philip Patston, Dr Peter Reagan, Professor Udo Schuklenk, Dr Libby Smales, Dr Frank Spring, Professor John Weaver and others. Between them they created one of the most exhaustive reviews of evidence on assisted dying ever assembled, in my opinion only rivalled by that found in *Carter v Canada*.

The contributions of the Human Rights Commission before and since the case have been tremendous. I am grateful for Matthew Palmer's work in the High Court, and the work of Janet Anderson-Bidois, Jackie Blue, Paul Gibson and the many other staff at the commission for their work in preparing their submission to the Health Select Committee this year.

I am extremely thankful for the case mounted by the team at Russell McVeagh, led by Dr Andrew Butler and Chris Curran. No one could have presented a better case. They were ably supported by Lecretia's dear friend and mine, Catherine Marks, and a team of bright young solicitors, including Olivia Bouchier, Mark Campbell, Matt Dodd, Owen Jaques, Matt McMenamin, David Smith, Ella Watt and Esther Watt. Katharine McGhie and Aidan Cameron, also at Russell McVeagh, were a huge help too. It was good to be able to commiserate with my friend Roger Shepherd, Catherine Marks' husband, who was working hard to complete his book while I was still working on mine.

It might surprise some but I am also thankful for the work of the office of the attorney-general, Christopher Finlayson, the solicitor-general, Mike Heron, and his associate counsel Paul Rishworth. During the case, as timelines were negotiated and embargoes agreed, they worked with the team at Russell McVeagh respectfully and generously, taking into account the urgency imposed by Lecretia's illness. If they hadn't done that, she might never have heard the judgment.

That she did see a judgment was down to the herculean efforts of Justice David Collins, who worked non-stop over the Queen's Birthday weekend after the hearing to deliver a judgment as quickly as possible. Although the judgment that was delivered was not the one Lecretia wanted, it was a miracle that it was delivered to her at all.

I am grateful for the help of my friends Emma Beals, Paul Brillinger, Aran Brown and Colleen Bermingham-Brown, Belinda Bundy, Jackie Garcia Cano, Kaila Colbin, Erin Connolly, Antonia Fattizzi, Hadley and Philip Fierlinger, Sara Goepel and Lucinda McFadden, Andrew Hovey, Larissa Paris, Richard Phillips, Tobin Postma, Zoë Prebble, Pamela Puchalski, Ronan Quirke, C. M. Samala, Paul Schrader, Ross Stanley, Julie Trell and Reina Webster-Iti, who all at various times offered moral support and encouragement during the writing of this book. Many of Lecretia's friends too, now mine, continued to support me after Lecretia passed away, including Alison and Jeremy Arthur-Young, Jon Black and Alice Boultbee, Giles Brown and Virginia Keast, Hilary Carr, David Friar and Barrie Connor, Kim and Mike Herrick, Sonya and Rob Hill,

Peter Jones, Rachael McConnell and Richard Murphy, Lucy McGrath and her parents John and Christine, Eileen McNaughton, Juliet Philpott and Andrew Smith, Christine Robertson and her parents Bruce and Lyn, Helen Salisbury and Tony Spellacey, Andrew and Abigail Skelton, and Prue Tyler.

Angela and Ben O'Meara deserve special mention for their attentiveness and help during Lecretia's illness and afterwards. Megan and Michael Huddleston were always there when Lecretia or I needed help and they were the best neighbours one could hope for. Rachel Hayward and Peter Fenton were incredibly supportive during Lecretia's illness and beyond. And Tim Clarke and Samantha Warner's support and true friendship have always been more generous and gracious than Lecretia or I ever hoped for or deserved.

Dame Jenny Gibbs was a great help in her support of Lecretia, incredibly generous with her time, as was her daughter, Debbi Gibbs, who along with Brian Sweeney, Catherine and Craig Walker, and Gerard van Bohemen, provided me with a warm welcome to New York. Pam Oliver and Kathryn Tucker also provided good advice and support.

John Burrows' eulogy at Lecretia's funeral was incredibly moving and wonderfully respectful. She adored

John and his friendship and would have been humbled to have known that he spoke.

Lecretia's friendship with Sir Geoffrey Palmer and his wife, Margaret, was one she treasured greatly, and I treasure it too. Sir Geoffrey and Margaret have always been generous with their time and their home, despite the many responsibilities that Sir Geoffrey carries even now, when most men his age would probably be choosing something very quiet to do. Lecretia regarded Sir Geoffrey as her mentor, and she could not have hoped for a better one.

Cate Brett deserves special mention for her unwavering friendship and support of Lecretia at the Law Commission, and then through her illness and beyond. It was Cate who prepared Lecretia and me for the demands of public life, and if we carried ourselves well at all, it was through her guidance.

Many politicians, old and new, have supported Lecretia, or at the very least the things she believed in. Michael Laws and Peter Brown were brave in bringing this issue before the house in 1995 and 2003 retrospectively, and although Maryan Street and Iain Lees-Galloway did not manage to get a bill before the house in their time, their efforts ensured the issue stayed in the public eye.

A big thank you to Christopher Bishop, Kevin Hague, Nikki Kaye, David Seymour, James Shaw,

Metiria Turei and Louisa Wall for all of their help inside and outside parliament. Thanks also to John Key for his brave public statements of support, given his position and the contentiousness of the issue, and to David Carter for making sure the issue was given the chance to be heard by the House. Thank you to Andrew Little for serendipitously though unintentionally providing the catalyst for *Seales v Attorney-General*, along with Kevin and Louisa, Jacqui Dean, Annette King, Barbara Kuriger, Simon O'Connor, Dr Shane Reti, Scott Simpson, Barbara Stewart and Poto Williams, for allowing the issue to be investigated by the Health Select Committee.

Finally I wish to thank the many thousands of Lecretia's supporters, including Don Brash, Andrew Denton, Helen Kelly, Gareth Morgan, Dave Mullan and David Stephens, who spoke out on the issue, wrote letters to MPs, signed the petition, made submissions to the Health Select Committee, or liked, commented on or shared posts on Lecretia's Facebook page, adding to the groundswell of popular support for change. One day, I truly believe that all those contributions will result in a change that Lecretia would have been proud of. For the sake of those living with terminal illnesses, I hope that day comes soon.